RECORDED VERSIONS GUITAR

AUTHENTIC TRANSCRIPTIONS WITH NOTES & TABLATURE

STEVIE RAY VAUGHAN
LIGHTNIN' BLUES 1983 – 1987

2nd Edition

Music transcriptions by Jesse Gress

Front Cover Photo — Copyright © 1986 John T. Comerford III
Photos on pages 1, 4 and Back Cover by Kim Upton

HAL•LEONARD®
CORPORATION

7777 W. BLUEMOUND RD. P.O. BOX 13819 MILWAUKEE, WI 53213

Visit Hal Leonard Online at
www.halleonard.com

STEVIE RAY VAUGHAN

LIGHTININ' BLUES 1983 – 1987

CONTENTS

STEVIE RAY VAUGHAN'S GUITAR STYLE

Stevie Ray Vaughan, born in Oak Cliff, Texas, which is a suburb of Dallas, was a star created from the blues revival of the '80s. His sound reflected a combination of Chicago, British and Texas blues styles. (Vaughan grew up in Texas where the blues has a meaner, tougher, harsher edge.) His playing also combined the essence of rock, country, jazz and swing styles. Vaughan began playing guitar at home in Dallas under the influence of his brother Jimmie (of the Fabulous Thunderbirds). He played in a number of bands in his teens—the Chantones, Blackbird and the Nightcrawlers. When he left high school in the ninth grade, he moved to Austin and played with the well-known local band, the Cobras. Later, in the mid-1970s, he formed his own ambitious blues-flavored/R&B band, Triple Threat. In 1981, Vaughan recruited drummer Chris Layton and bassist Tommy Shannon and formed Double Trouble (taken from the name of an Otis Rush song). Their reputation soon grew to such proportions that the band was invited to the 1982 Montreux Festival in Switzerland. A *People* magazine review stated that "…they reduced the stage to a pile of ashes." Offers came in and their debut album, *Texas Flood*, recorded under the direction of veteran producer John Hammond, was released on Epic. In the summer of '83, it cracked *Billboard's* Top 40 albums. Stevie's music was on its way to the international prominence it holds today.

Blues players especially important to Vaughan included Eric Clapton, Albert King, Otis Rush, Jimi Hendrix, B.B. King, T-Bone Walker, Freddie King, Buddy Guy, Howlin' Wolf and fellow Texan, Albert Collins. Many of his songs spotlight the styles of these great performers, such as "Come On" (an Earl King song also covered by Hendrix) and Vaughan's unique version of "Voodoo Chile," a homage to Hendrix with a harsh, soulful blues/rock sound. Vaughan's been an inspiration to many guitarists, eschewing the two-handed techniques and tricks of the '80s and instead, building his own style in the roots of the blues.

Listen to the jazzy swing feel to the songs "Stangs Swang" and "Gone Home," and you'll know that Vaughan also cited Django Reinhardt as an influence. But it's Vaughan's own volcanic playing and knowledge of his instrument that's such a knockout. As a news reviewer phrased it, "He can play it at the speed of light, sustain a note for days, and he knows how to get every sound—*every sound*—possible out of his guitar." He's also been touted as one of the finest singers in the blues-rock vein and one of the most devoutly committed to his style and art. The albums covered is this book have gone gold and garnered many Grammy nominations and awards. In addition, Vaughan can be heard on several other well-known artist's albums including David Bowie's *Lets Dance* and Brian Slawson's *Distant Drums*, and on the soundtracks of motion pictures including, *Gung Ho*, *Rocky IV*, *I Live in America*, and *Back to the Beach* where he appeared playing his own version of "Pipeline."

Tuning

Because he liked the sound (and to facilitate string-bending), Vaughan tuned his guitar down a half-step:
1st string E to E♭
2nd string B to B♭
3rd string G to G♭
4th string D to D♭
5th string A to A♭
6th string E to E♭

His bassist, Tommy Shannon, also tunes down a half-step. Vaughan sometimes played a Hamiltone guitar with an inch longer fingerboard, in which the strings are still the same pitch as if he was tuned in E.

Open String Riffs

Open string riffs give a twangy, Texas, country rock feel to songs like "Scuttle Buttin'", "Love Struck Baby," and "Voodoo Child (Slight Return)."

The Jimi Hendrix screaming metal blues style is expressed on Vaughan's cover of "Voodoo Child (Slight Return)", and his own interpretation of the Hendrix style is also heard on "Life Without You" and "Come On (Part III)."

The E Blues Scale

The E blues (1-♭3-4-♭5-5-♭7-8) is used throughout many of Vaughan's songs.

Here is an example in "Pride and Joy" of his use of the flat 5 in a riff that uses all the notes of an E blues scale in an inverted fashion.

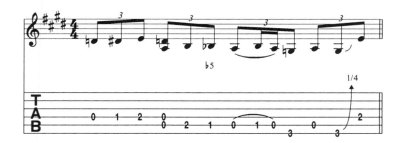

Alternate Picking

Vaughan uses a heavy down stroke on the bass line notes and a light upstroke, usually consisting of a chord or muted strings.

Combined bass and rhythm lines on "Pride and Joy"

The Dorian Mode

The A Dorian scale is used quite frequently by Vaughan. The flat 3/C and the flat 7/G give a minor sounding flavor to a song like "Willy the Wimp." However in this book, there are places where the key signature of G (one sharp) has been used instead of A (three sharps) to decrease the use of accidentals and make the transcriptions easier to read.

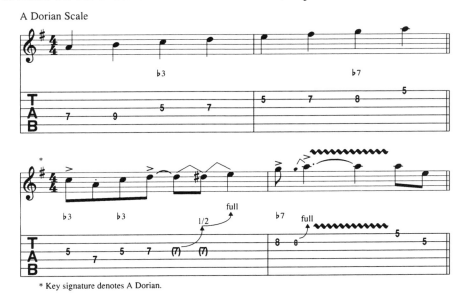

* Key signature denotes A Dorian.

Common Riffs

Intervals of 4ths are used for the introductions, as in "Love Struck Baby" and "Lookin' Out the Window," giving these songs a '50s rock 'n' roll feel.

Near the end of "Cold Shot," Vaughan uses an E7♯9 chord, frantically alternating between the bass root note E and the body of the chord (G♯, D, F✕ [F double sharp] and B) to create a climactic tension within the final moments of the song.

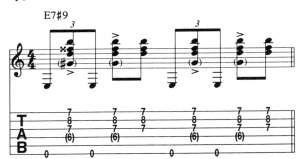

"Texas Flood" is written in 12/8 to emphasize the rolling, bluesy motion of the solos.

7

Chord Forms

The following chords are common in Vaughan's playing:

(A9 contains an interval of a major 2nd, because the ♭7 is in the bass.)

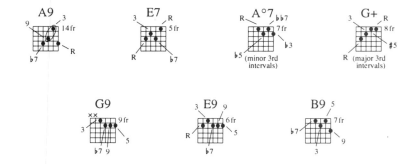

Shuffle Rhythms

The shuffle rhythms give a rock flavor to tunes such as "Look at Little Sister" and "Lookin' Out the Window."

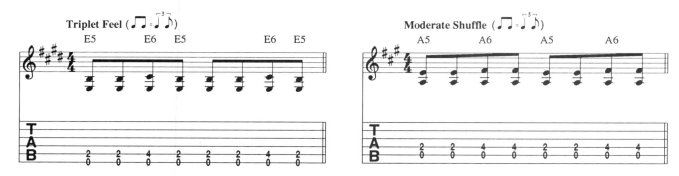

Equipment

Vaughan's "Number 1" guitar was his '59 Stratocaster with stock pickups, and a '61 left-handed neck. His collection is made up mainly of Strats (several with names such as *Charley* and *Lenny*). For instance, on "Honey Bee" he played a hollowed-out Strat, on "Gone Home" he played a Strat, on "Swang's Stang" he played a Johnny Smith model guitar, and on "Say What," Vaughan used two Vox wah-wah pedals, one of which was owned by Jimi Hendrix. Most of his guitars have bass frets—he liked the way they feel and found it easier to grip the strings. He used GHS strings, usually starting at .012 down to .058.

He played through Howard Dumble amps, Fender Vibroverbs, Super Reverbs and Marshall cabinets (this, of course, varied according to studio and performing situations).

Finale

The following transcriptions include material from *Texas Flood,* Vaughan's first album (recorded at Jackson Browne's studio), *Couldn't Stand the Weather,* a funky technical blues masterpiece, *Soul to Soul,* his tight, hit song-oriented third album, and *Live, Alive,* a collection of songs capturing his highly-charged concert sound.

These transcriptions provide an in-depth study of Stevie Ray Vaughan's playing. If you love the blues (the roots of rock and roll), you will find Vaughan has taken the soul and the sound of the blues one step further.

STEVIE RAY VAUGHAN

LIGHTININ' BLUES 1983 – 1987

DISCOGRAPHY

TEXAS FLOOD ....Epic, 1983
BLUES EXPLOSION (various artists) ....Atlantic, 1984
COULDN'T STAND THE WEATHER ....Epic, 1984
SOUL TO SOUL ....Epic, 1985
LIVE ALIVE ....Epic, 1986
IN STEP ....Epic, 1989
STRAWBERRY FIELDS (various artists) ....Columbia
FAMILY STYLE ....Epic, 1990
THE SKY IS CRYING ....Epic, 1991
IN THE BEGINNING ....Epic, 1992

STEVIE RAY VAUGHAN SOLO DISCOGRAPHY (various cuts)

LET'S DANCE/DAVID BOWIE...EMI/Manhattan, 1983
STRIKE LIKE LIGHTNING/LONNIE MACK
  (Stevie Ray Vaughan/Co-Producer ....Alligator, 1985
GRAVITY/JAMES BROWN ....Columbia, 1986
HEARTBEAT/DON JOHNSON ....Epic, 1986
EMERALD CITY/TEENA MARIE ....Epic, 1986
CHARACTERS/STEVIE WONDER ....Motown, 1987
FAMOUS BLUE RAINCOAT/JENNIFER WARNES ....Cypress, 1987
BACK TO THE BEACH/Various Artists ....Columbia, 1987
DISTANT DRUMS/BRIAN SLAWSON ....Columbia, 1988
I'M IN THE WRONG BUSINESS/A.C. REED.....................................Alligator, 1988
"BULL DURHAM"/Various Artists ....Capitol, 1988
MADRE DOLCISSIMA – JESUS/ADELMO FONACIARI ....Polygram (Italy), 1989

Dirty Pool

By Stevie Ray Vaughan and Doyle Bramhall

Tune Down 1/2 Step:
① = Eb ④ = Db
② = Bb ⑤ = Ab
③ = Gb ⑥ = Eb

Intro
Slow Blues ♩. = 52

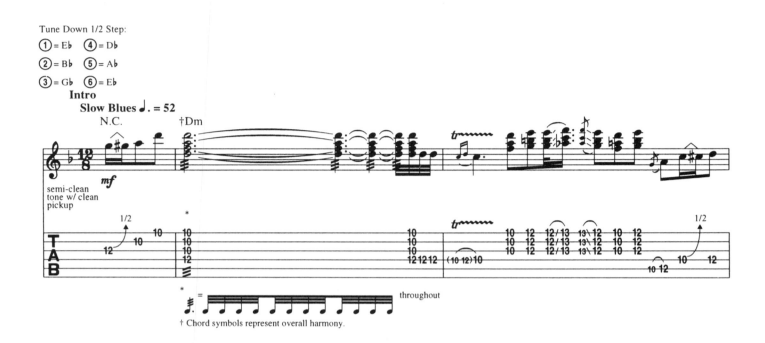

semi-clean
tone w/ clean
pickup

*♩. = ♩ throughout

† Chord symbols represent overall harmony.

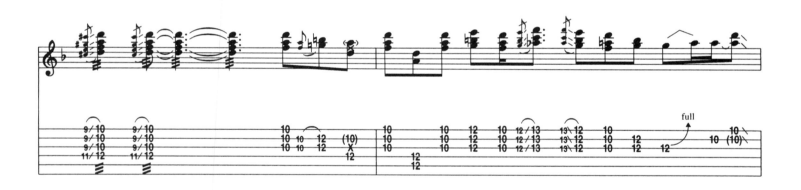

*T=Thumb

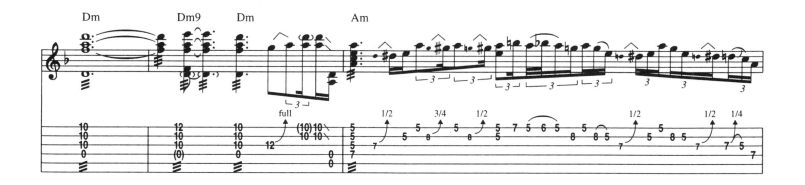

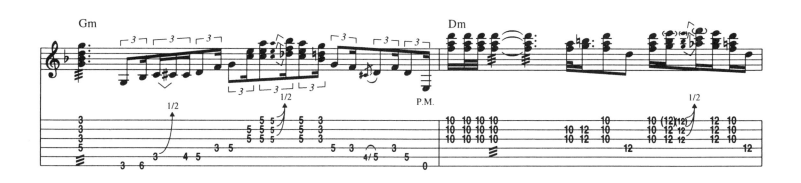

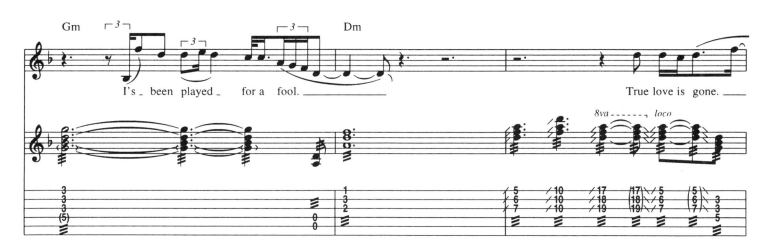

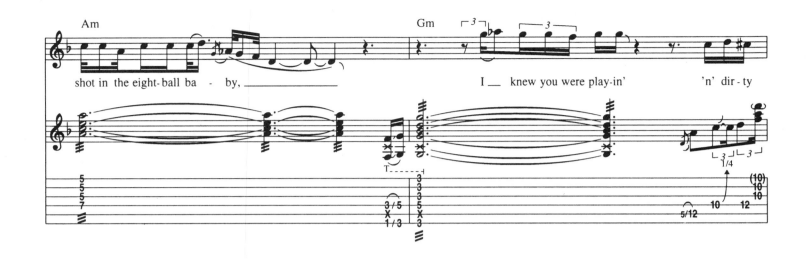

shot in the eight-ball ba - by, _____   I __ knew you were play-in'   'n' dir - ty

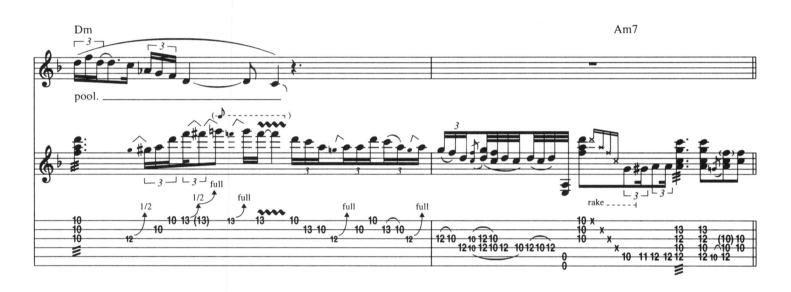

pool. _____

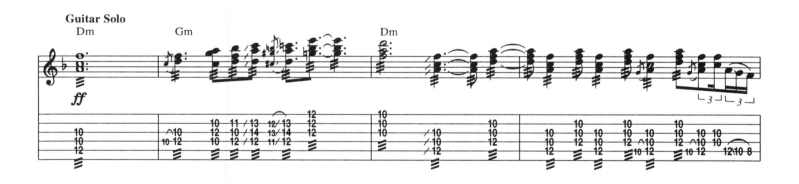

Guitar Solo

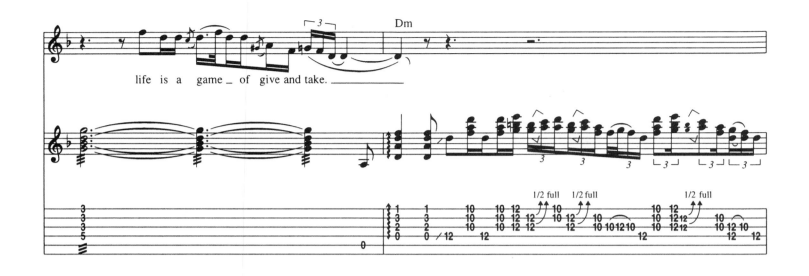

life is a game _ of give and take. _____

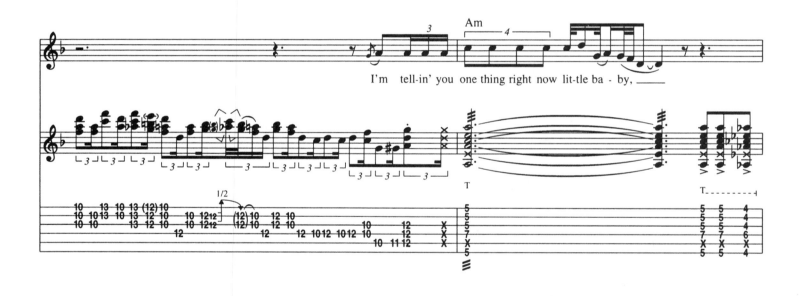

I'm tell-in' you one thing right now lit-tle ba - by, _____

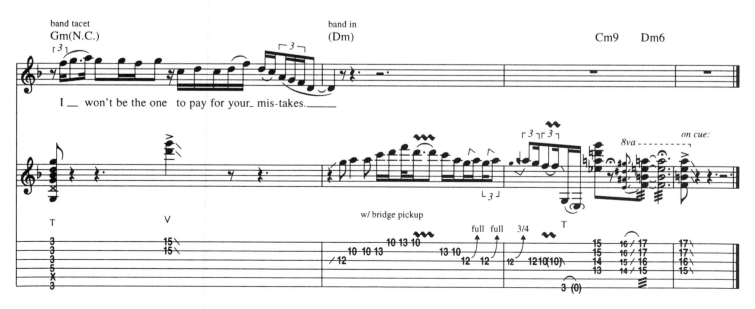

I _ won't be the one to pay for your _ mis-takes. _____

band tacet
Gm(N.C.)

band in
(Dm)

Cm9   Dm6

w/ bridge pickup

on cue:
8va

I'm Cryin'

By Stevie Ray Vaughan

* Chord symbols represent overall harmony.

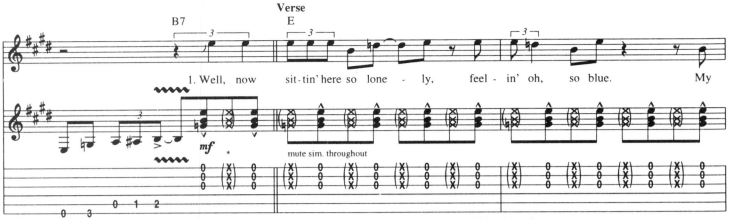

1. Well, now sit-tin' here so lone - ly, feel - in' oh, so blue. My

* Mute notes in parenthesis (x) by "patting" strings with palm of pick hand throughout.

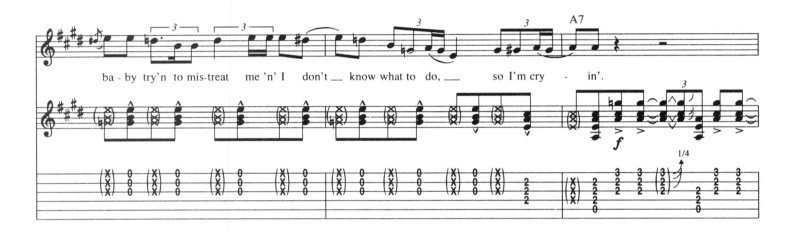

ba - by try'n to mis-treat me 'n' I don't __ know what to do, ___ so I'm cry - in'.

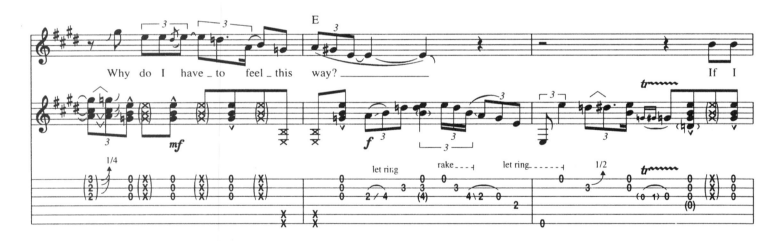

Why do I have __ to feel __ this way? _____ If I

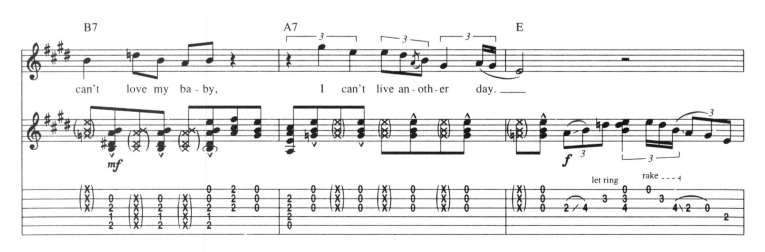

can't love my ba - by, I can't live an - oth-er day. ___

Guitar Solo

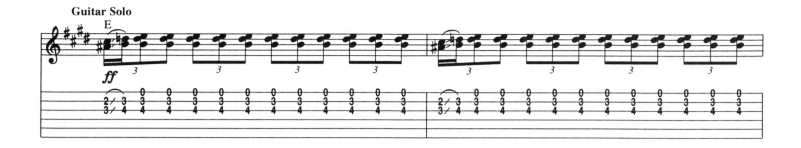

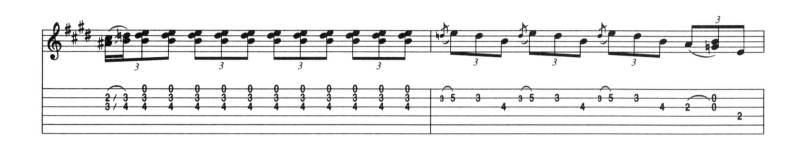

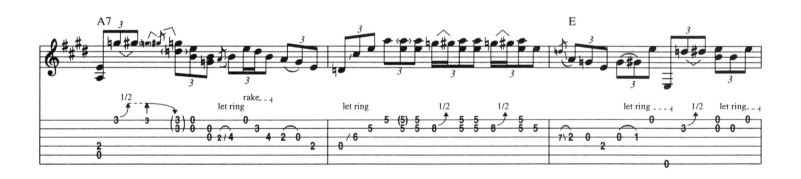

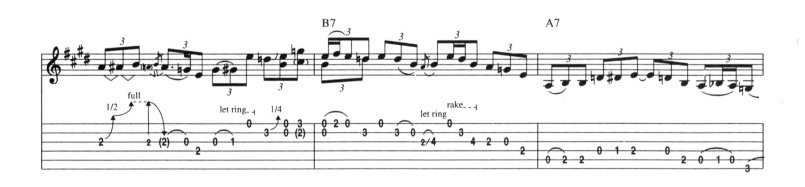

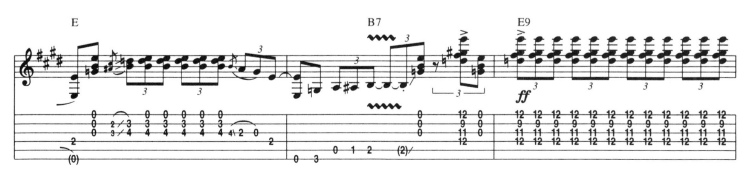

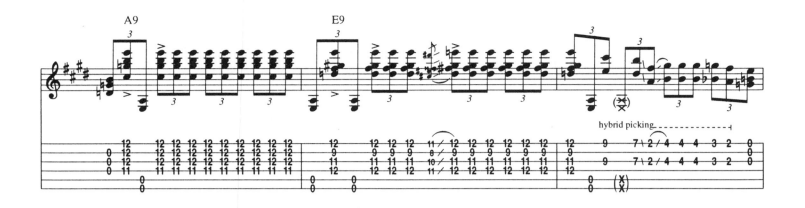

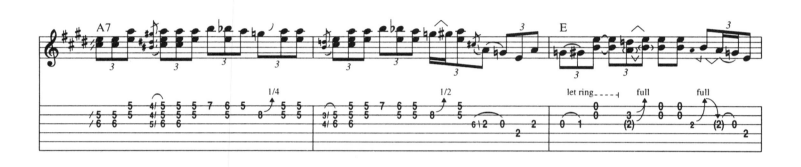

4. Yeah, now when I first met you ba - by, ev - 'ry -

thing seemed to be fine. But now when we're to-geth-er yeah, __ it's a to-tal waste of time, __ so I'm cry-

-in'. Why do I have __ to feel __ this way? _____

If I can't love ya, ba-by, I can't live an-oth-er day. .

_____ 5. Well, __ I guess it's just my own __ fault, __ the

truth I can not hide. ___ If I ev - er get you back ___ a-gain, then I'll stay ___ right by your side, I won't be cry -

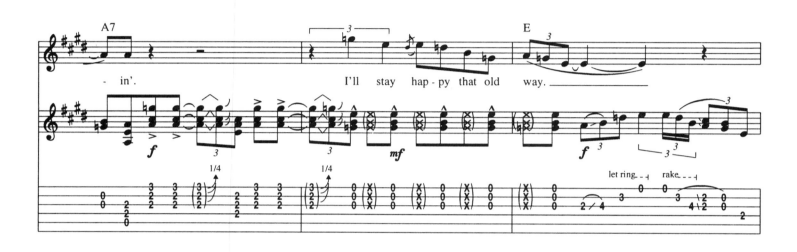

- in'. I'll stay hap - py that old way. _____

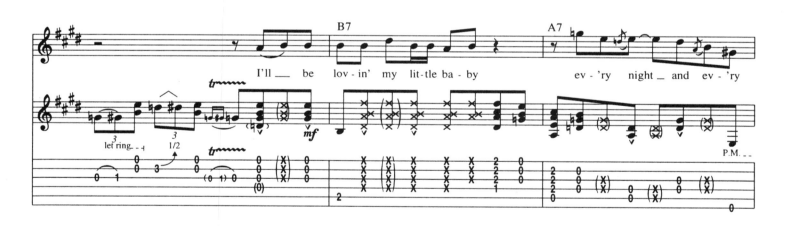

I'll ___ be lov - in' my lit-tle ba - by ev - 'ry night ___ and ev - 'ry

Guitar Solo

day. _____

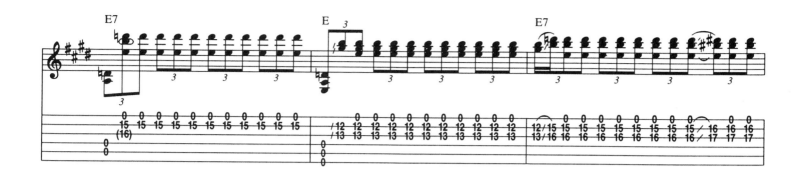

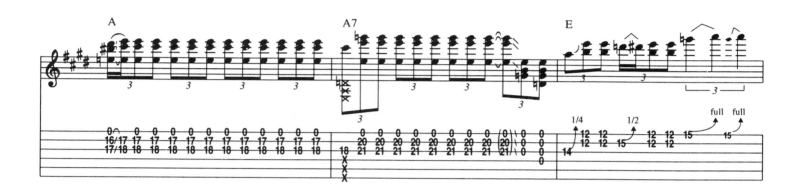

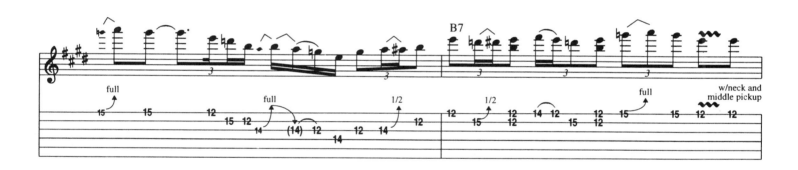

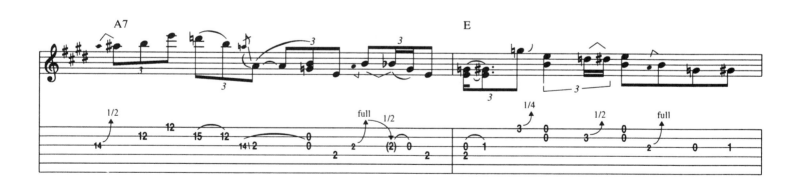

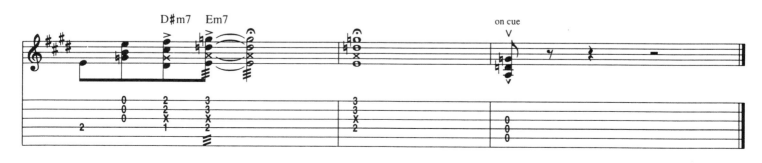

Love Struck Baby

Words and Music by Stevie Ray Vaughan

Tune Down 1/2 Step:
① = E♭ ④ = D♭
② = B♭ ⑤ = A♭
③ = G♭ ⑥ = E♭

1. Well, I'm a love struck ba-by, I ___ must con-fess. ___ Life ___ with-out you dar-ling's just a sol-id mess. ___ Think-in' 'bout you ba-by give me such a thrill, ___ I got-ta have you, mm ba-by, can't ___ get my fill. ___ I ___ love you ba-by, an' I know just what to do. ___

Pre-Chorus

I ____ still re-mem-ber, an' let it be said, __ the way you make me feel it'll take a

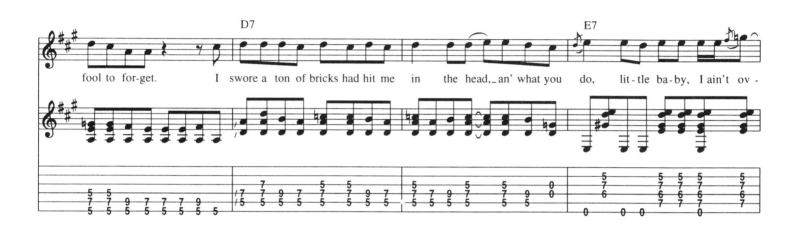

fool to for-get. I swore a ton of bricks had hit me in the head,__ an' what you do, lit-tle ba-by, I ain't ov -

- er it yet. Ev-'ry time I see you, make me feel so fine. __ Heart beat-in' cra-zy, my blood__

__ is run-nin' wild. Lov-in' makes me feel like a might-y, might-y man. Love __ me __ ba-by, ain't I __

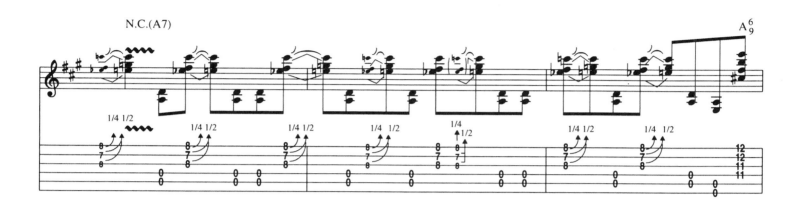

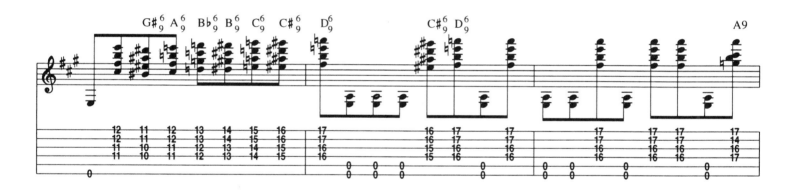

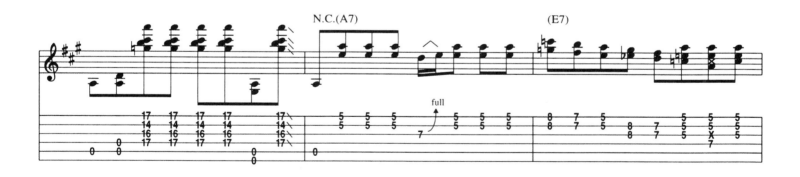

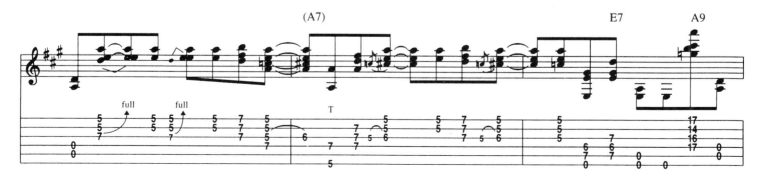

Sparks start fly-in' ev-'ry time we meet. ___ Let me tell you ba-by, you knock me off my feet. Your

Mary Had A Little Lamb

By George B. Guy (a/k/a Buddy Guy)

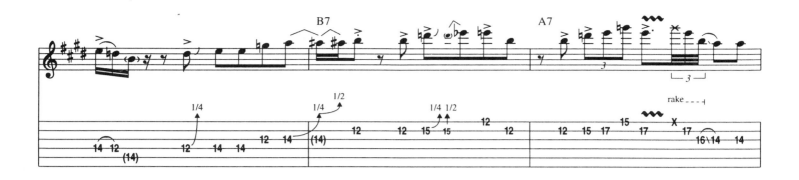

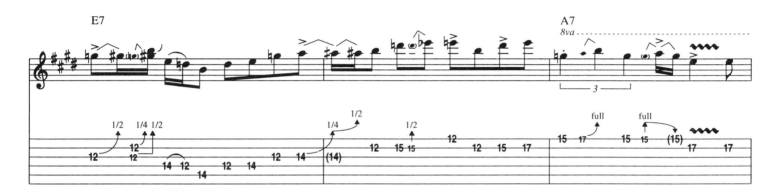

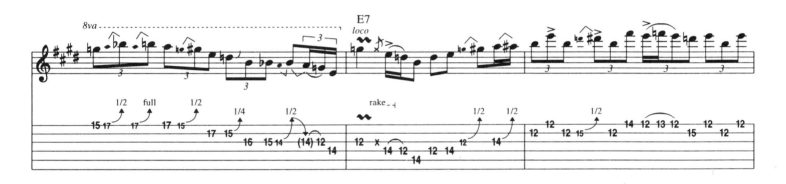

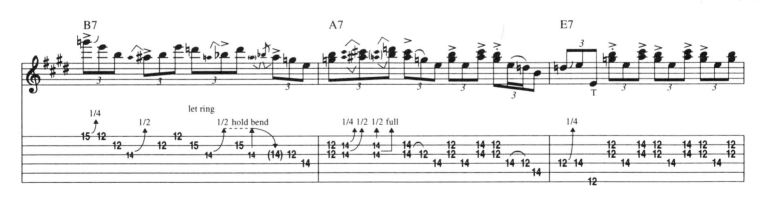

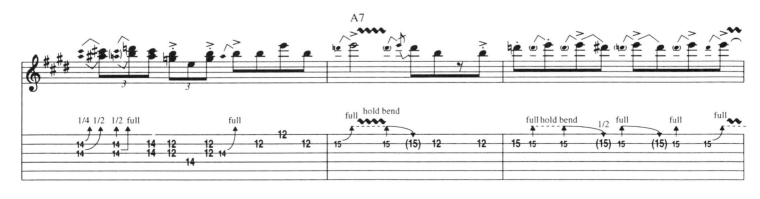

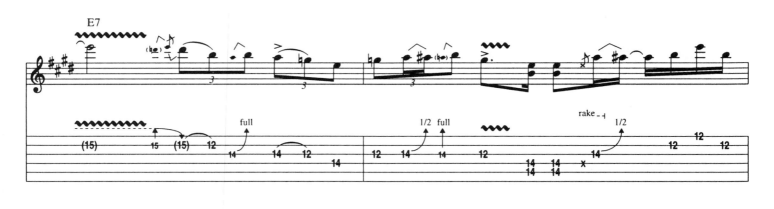

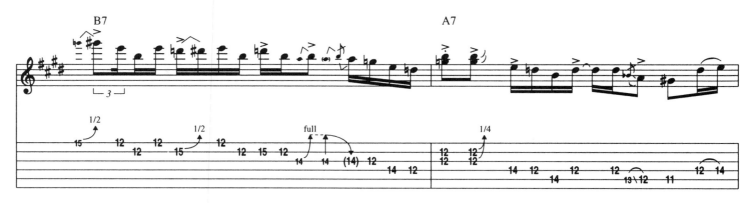

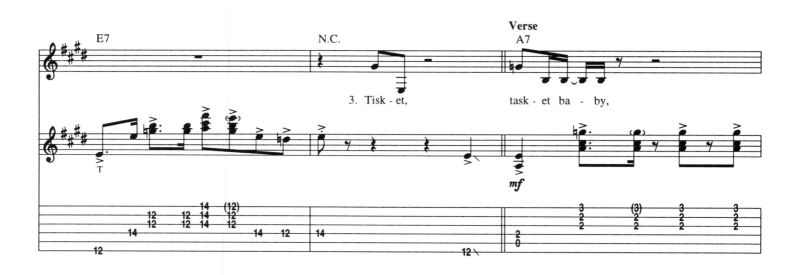

3. Tisk - et,   task - et ba - by,

a green 'n' yel - low __ bas - ket. __   Sent a   let - ter to   my

ba - by, _____ an' on my way I passed ___ it. ___

Outro

Pride And Joy

By Stevie Ray Vaughan

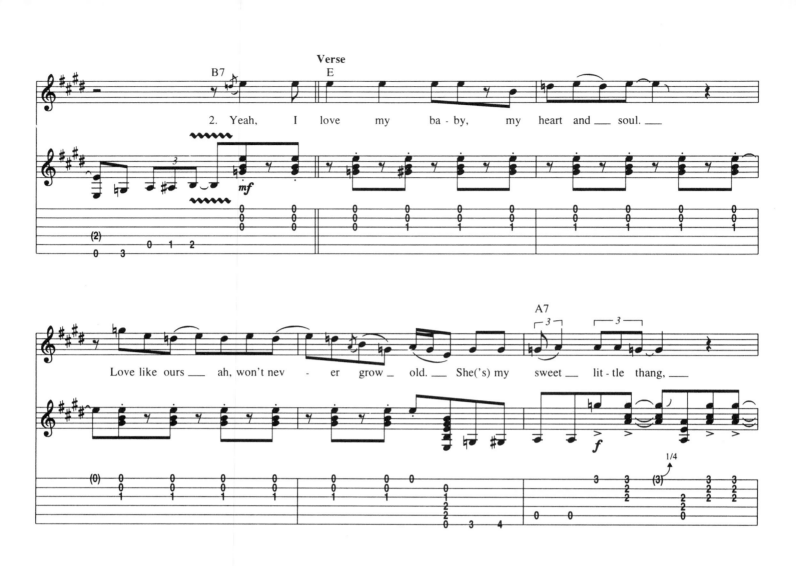

Verse

2. Yeah, I love my ba - by, my heart and ___ soul. ___

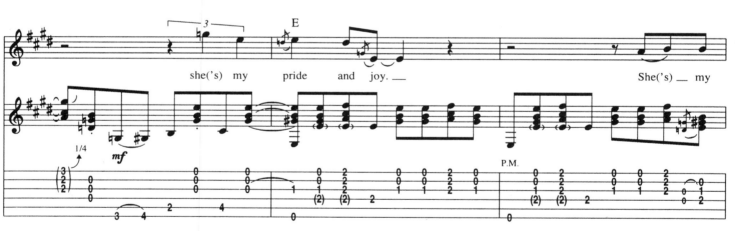

Love like ours ___ ah, won't nev - er grow ___ old. ___ She('s) my sweet ___ lit - tle thang, ___

she('s) my pride and joy. ___ She('s) ___ my

sweet lit - tle ba - by, I'm ___ her ___ lit - tle lov - er boy. ___

sweet _ lit-tle ba - by, I'm _ her _ lit-tle lov-er boy. _

Guitar Solo

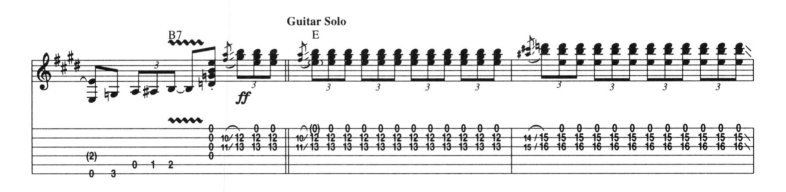

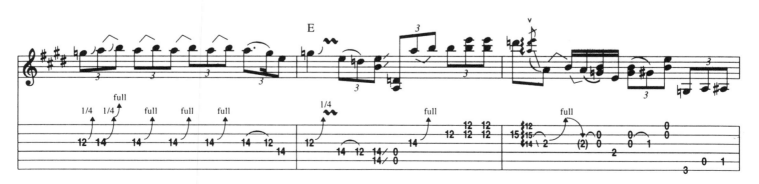

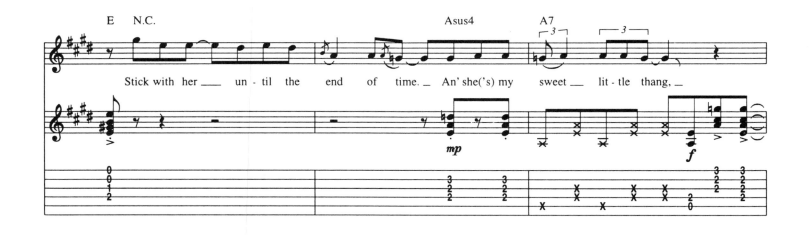

Stick with her ___ un - til the end of time. ___ An' she('s) my sweet ___ lit - tle thang, ___

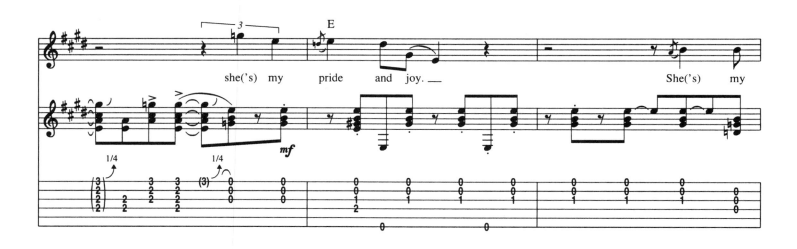

she('s) my pride and joy. ___ She('s) my

sweet lit - tle ba - by, I'm ___ her ___ lit - tle lov - er boy. ___

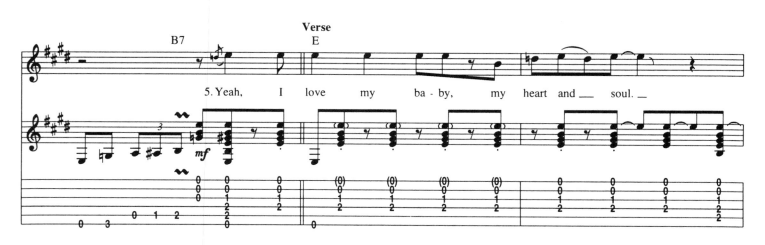

Verse

5. Yeah, I love my ba - by, my heart and ___ soul. ___

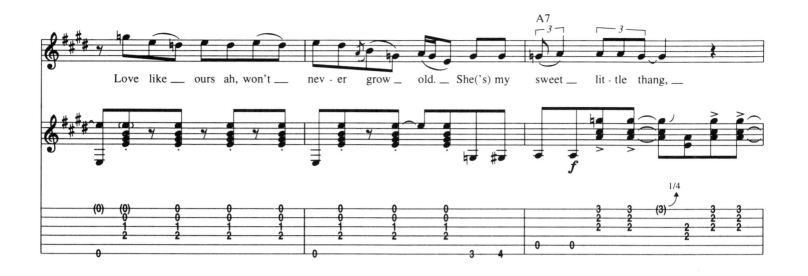

Love like ___ ours ah, won't ___ nev - er grow ___ old. She('s) my sweet ___ lit - tle thang, ___

she('s) my pride and joy. ___ She('s) ___ my

sweet lit-tle ba - by, I'm ___ her ___ lit - tle lov - er boy. ___

Guitar Solo

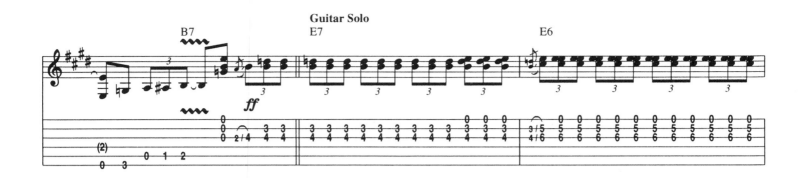

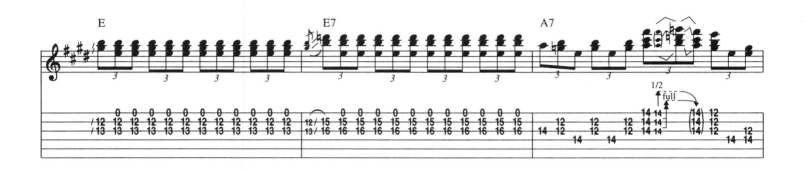

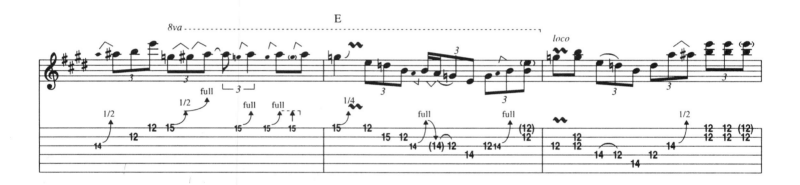

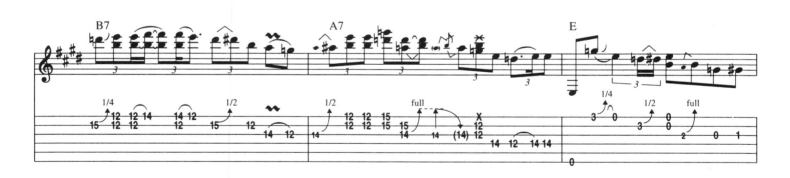

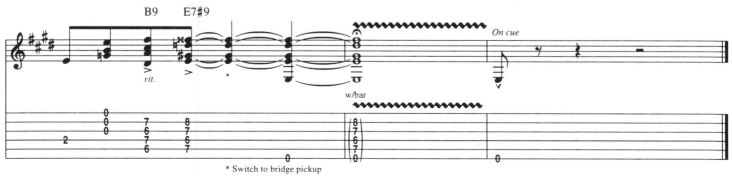

* Switch to bridge pickup

Texas Flood

Words and Music by Larry C. Davis and Joseph W. Scott

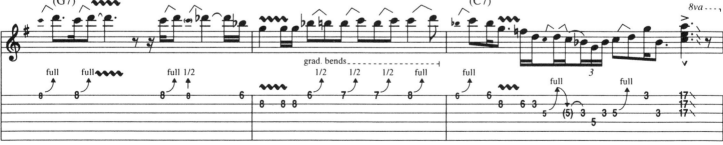

Verse

1. Well,_ it's flood-in' down in Tex-as._

All of the tel-e-phone lines _ are down. _

*T = thumb

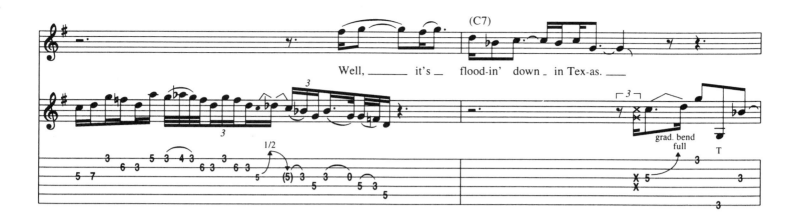

Well, _____ it's _____ flood-in' down _____ in Tex-as. _____

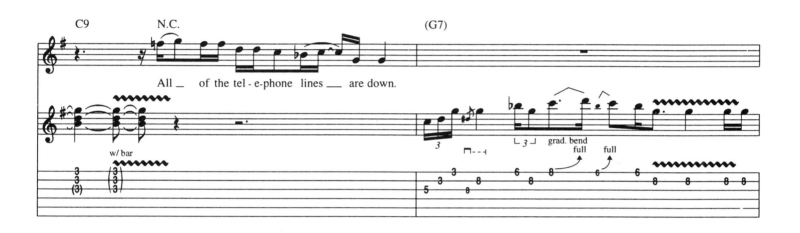

All __ of the tel - e-phone lines ____ are down.

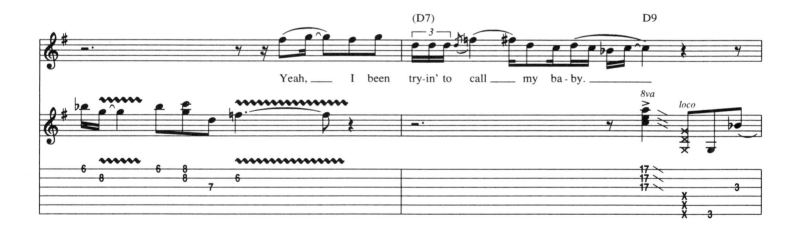

Yeah, ____ I been try-in' to call ____ my ba - by. _____

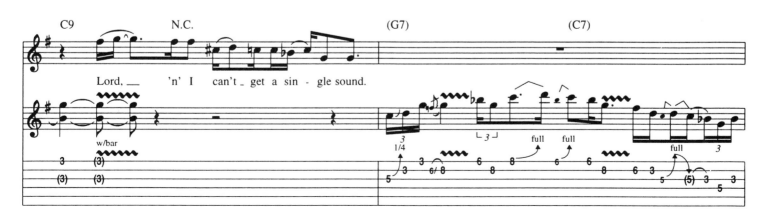

Lord, ___ 'n' I can't _ get a sin - gle sound.

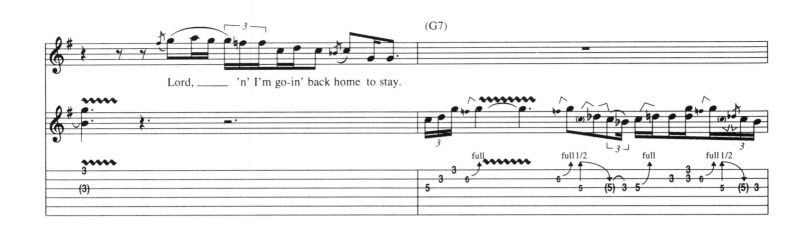

Lord, _____ 'n' I'm go-in' back home to stay.

Well, _ back home there's no _____ floods or tor - na - does,

babe, _____ 'n' the _ sun shines _ ev - 'ry day. _____

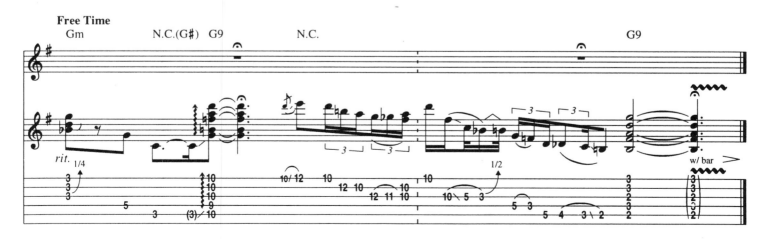

Cold Shot

By Mike Kindred and W. C. Clark

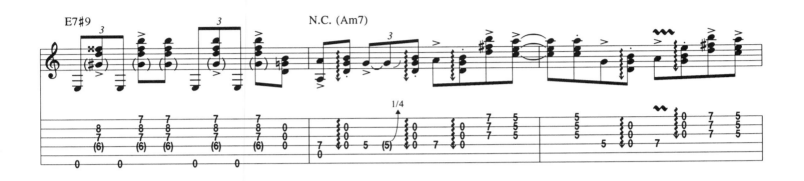

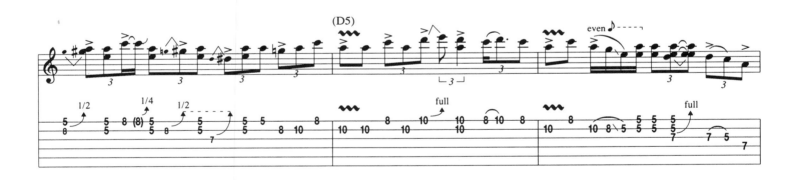

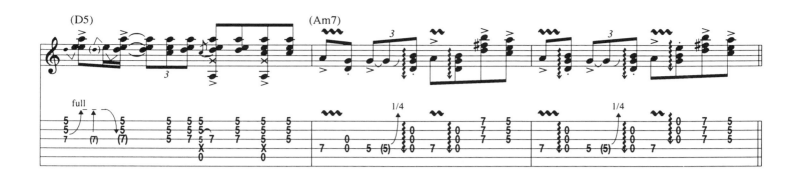

Verse

3. I __ real-ly meant I was sor - ry for ev-er caus-in' you pain. _____

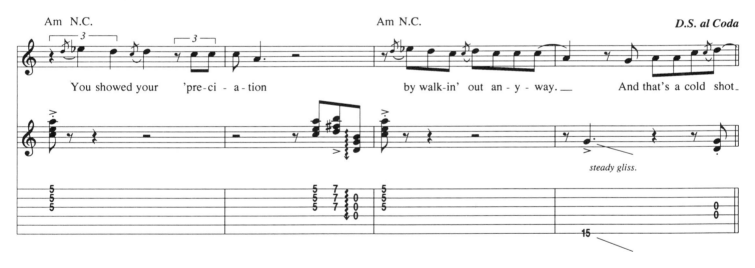

You showed your 'pre-ci - a-tion by walk-in' out an-y-way. __ And that's a cold shot_

steady gliss.

⊕ Coda

Couldn't Stand The Weather

By Stevie Ray Vaughan

* Key signature indicates D Mixolydian.
** Arpeggiate and strum chords freely.

Gtr. 2: w/ Riff A, 4 times

* T=Thumb on ⑥

wash a - way.   Rain   or   shine,   it's al - ways   here   to   stay.   All   these   years,   you 'n' I've

spent to - geth - er,   all   this,   we   just   could - n't stand the weath - er.

2. Like a train that stops at ev-'ry sta-tion, __ we __ all deal __ with trials __

__ and trib-u-la - tions. Fear hangs the fel-low that ties up his years, __

en-tan-gled in yel-low and cries __ all his tears. Chang-es come __ be-fore we can go. __

Learn to see them be - fore ___ we're too old. ___ Don't just take me for

try'n' to be heav - y. Un-der-stand, ___ it's time to get r-read-y forthe storm. ___

Guitar Solo

Gtr. 2: w/ Rhy. Fig. 3, 6 1/2 times, simile

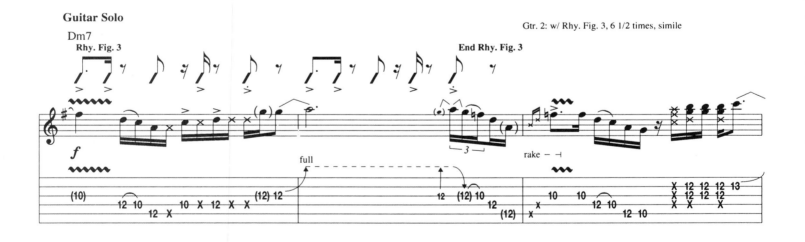

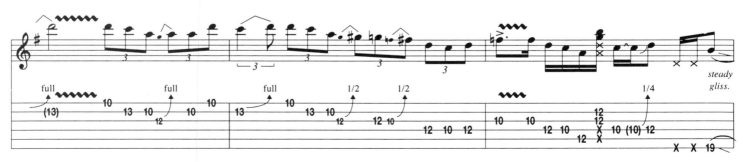

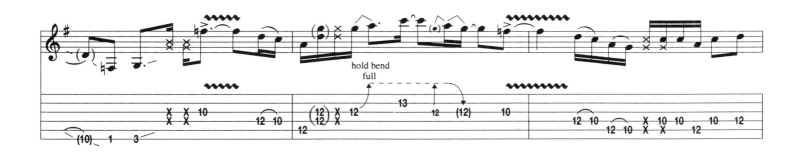

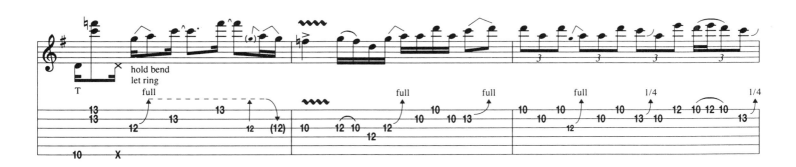

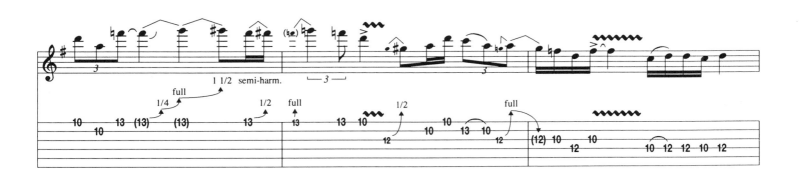

Gtr. 2: w/ Rhy. Fig. 2, simile

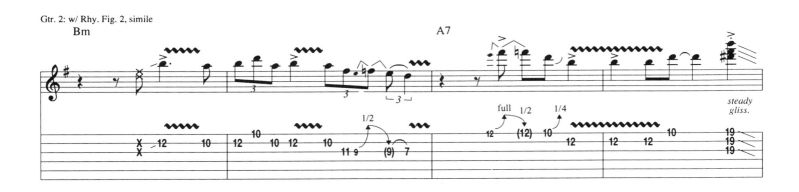

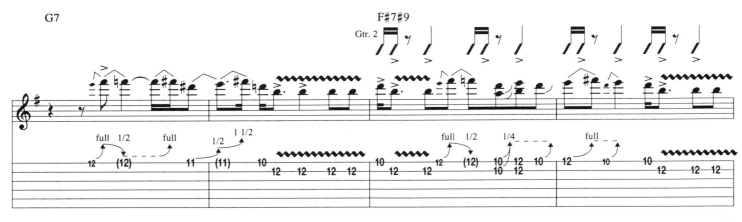

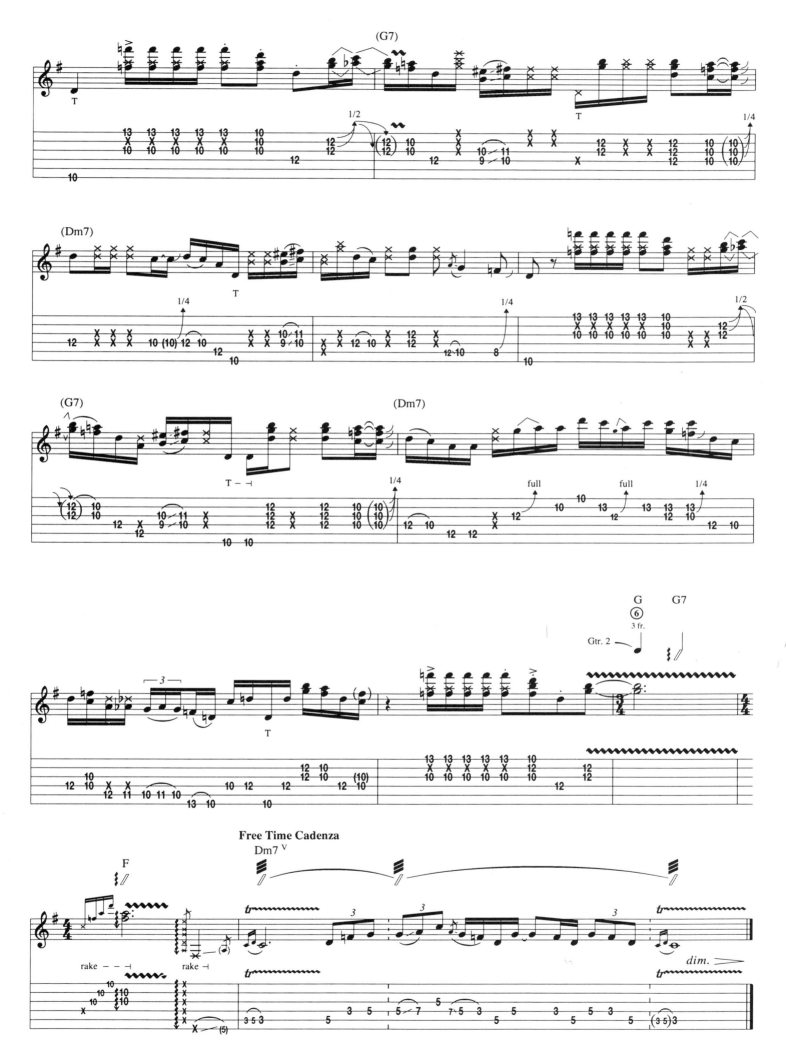

Honey Bee

By Stevie Ray Vaughan

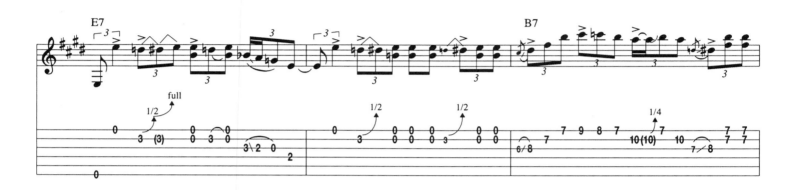

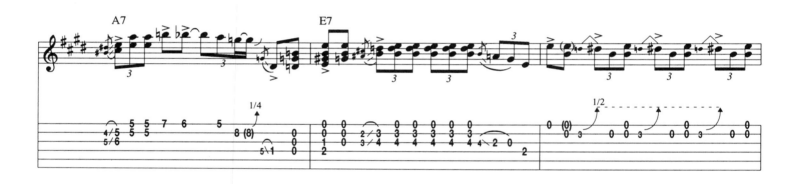

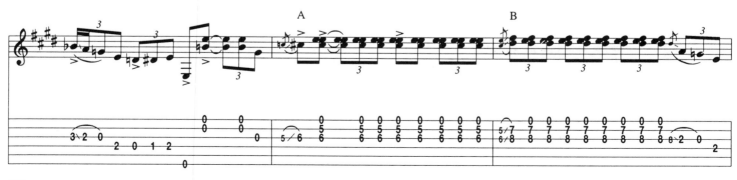

⊕ Coda

Outro Guitar Solo

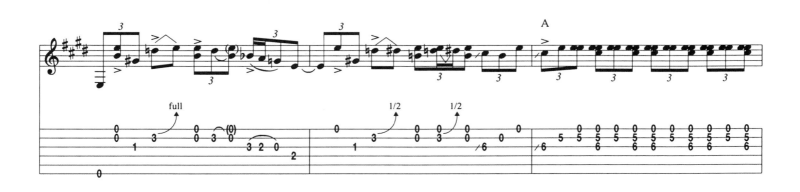

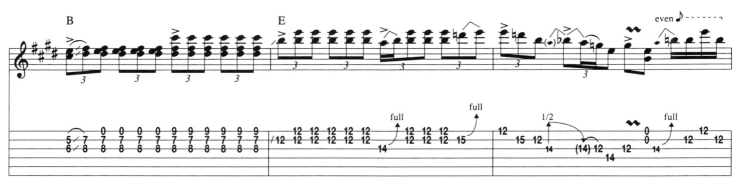

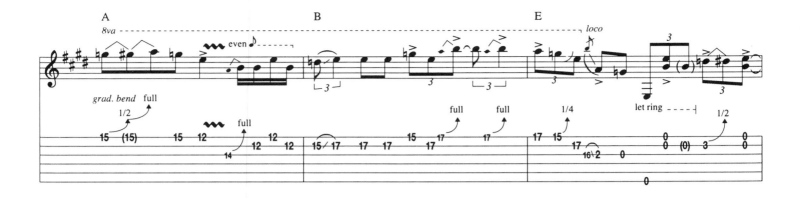

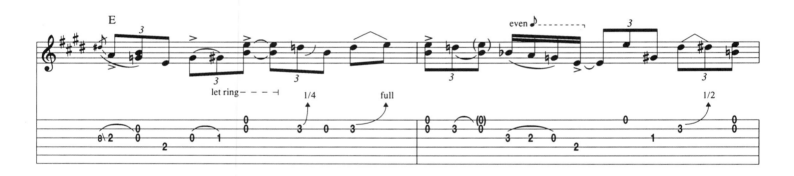

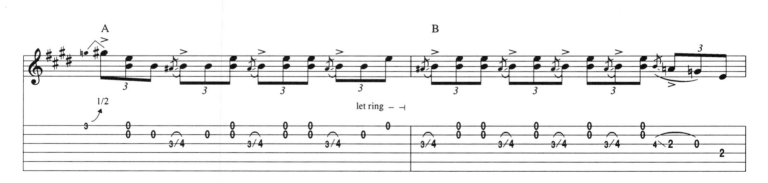

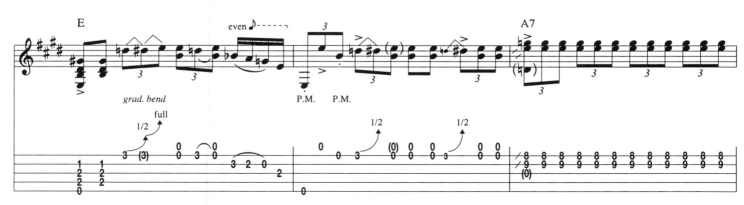

Scuttle Buttin'

By Stevie Ray Vaughan

Tune Down 1/2 Step:
①= Eb ④ = Db
②= Bb ⑤ = Ab
③ = Gb ⑥ = Eb

Moderately Fast ♩ = 160

Gtr. 1 (dist.)

N.C.

A Theme

* E7#9

f

* Chord symbols represent implied harmony.

N.C.

E7#9

full

N.C.

A7

full

N.C.

E7#9

full

N.C.

B7#9

full

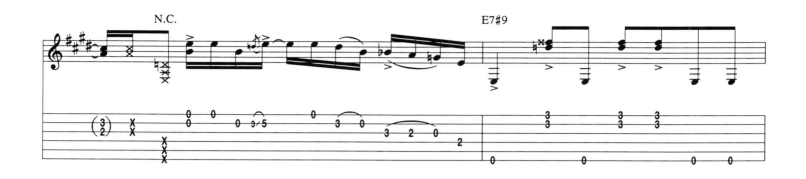

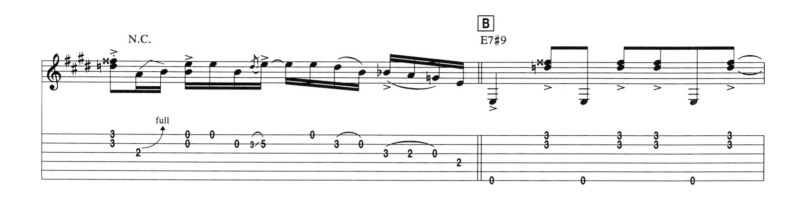

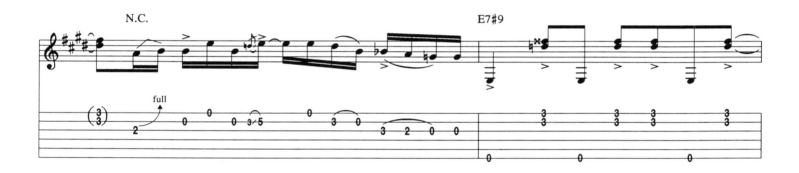

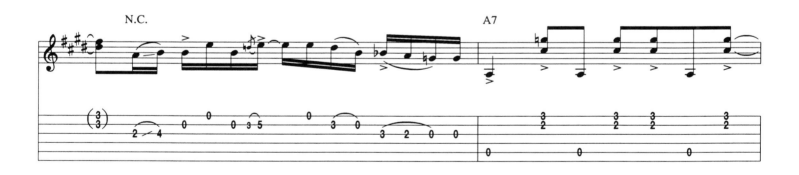

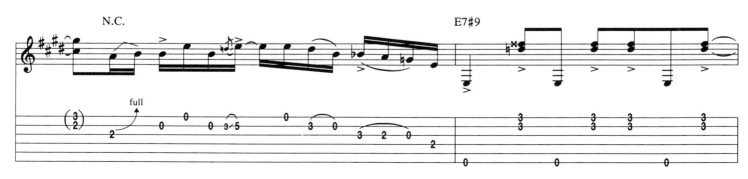

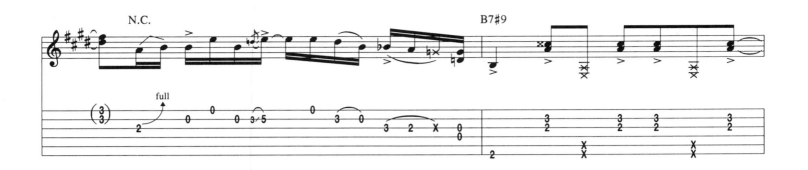

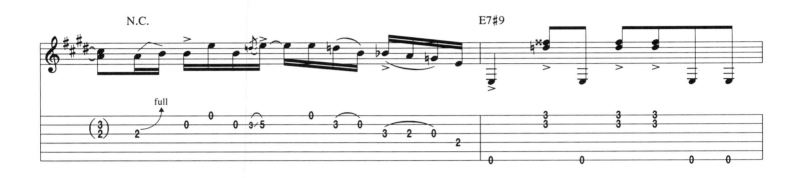

C Guitar Solo

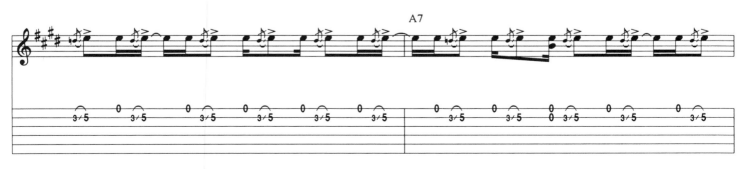

Stang's Swang

By Stevie Ray Vaughan

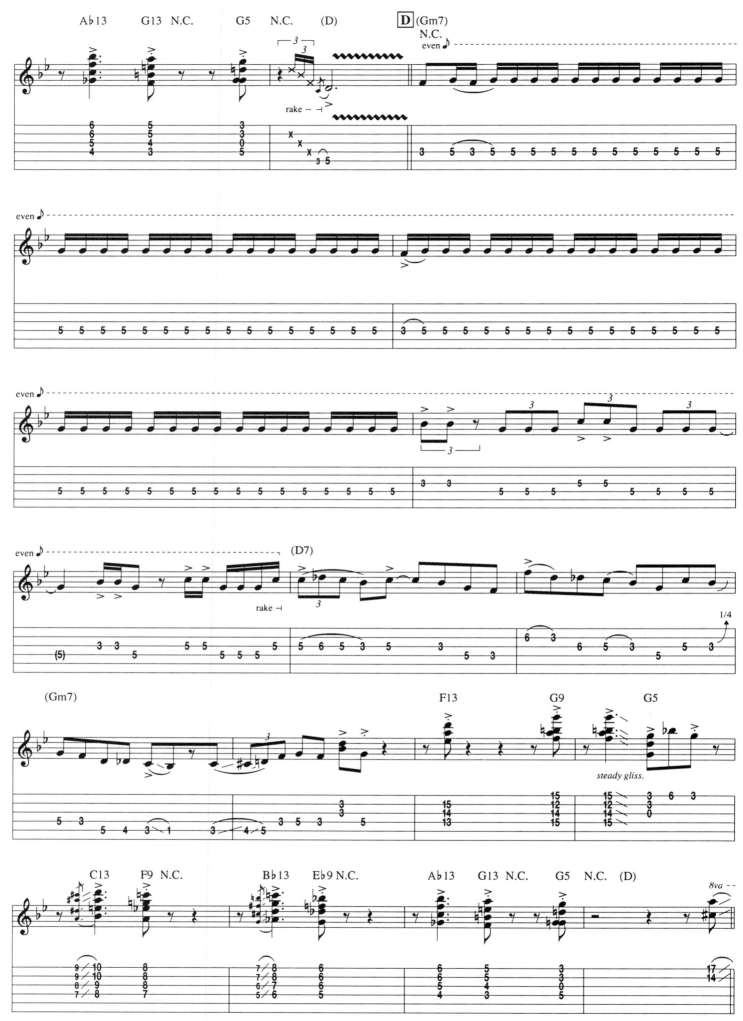

Voodoo Child (Slight Return)

Words and Music by Jimi Hendrix

Tune Down 1/2 Step:
① = Eb ④ = Db
② = Bb ⑤ = Ab
③ = Gb ⑥ = Eb

Intro
Moderately Slow ♩ = 94

Gtr. 1

N.C.

* w/ wah-wah & dist.

mp

* + = treble position (pedal down)
* o = bass position (pedal up)

mf
rake

1/4

* T = Thumb on ⑥

cont. w/ wah simile

1/4

(drums enter)

1/4

1/4

(band enter)

N.C.(E7#9)

wah off

f

1/2

full

1/2

Verse
(E7#9)
N.C.

1. Well, I'm stand-in' next to a moun-tain,   chop it down _ a-with the edge of my _

88

Verse
N.C.(E7♯9)

2. I did-n't mean to take up all your _ sweet time, _

(I'll) give it right back to ya   a-one o' these days.

I did-n't mean to take __ up all your sweet   time,

give it right back to ya   the rest o' my days.

Lord knows, I'm a voo-doo chile. _

Guitar Solo

N.C.(E7)

fuzz on   wah on   rake ⌐   w/ bar   ＜ fdbk.   rake ⌐

pitch: G

hold bend   ⌐ 3 ⌐   wah off

grad. bend   1/4   1 1/2

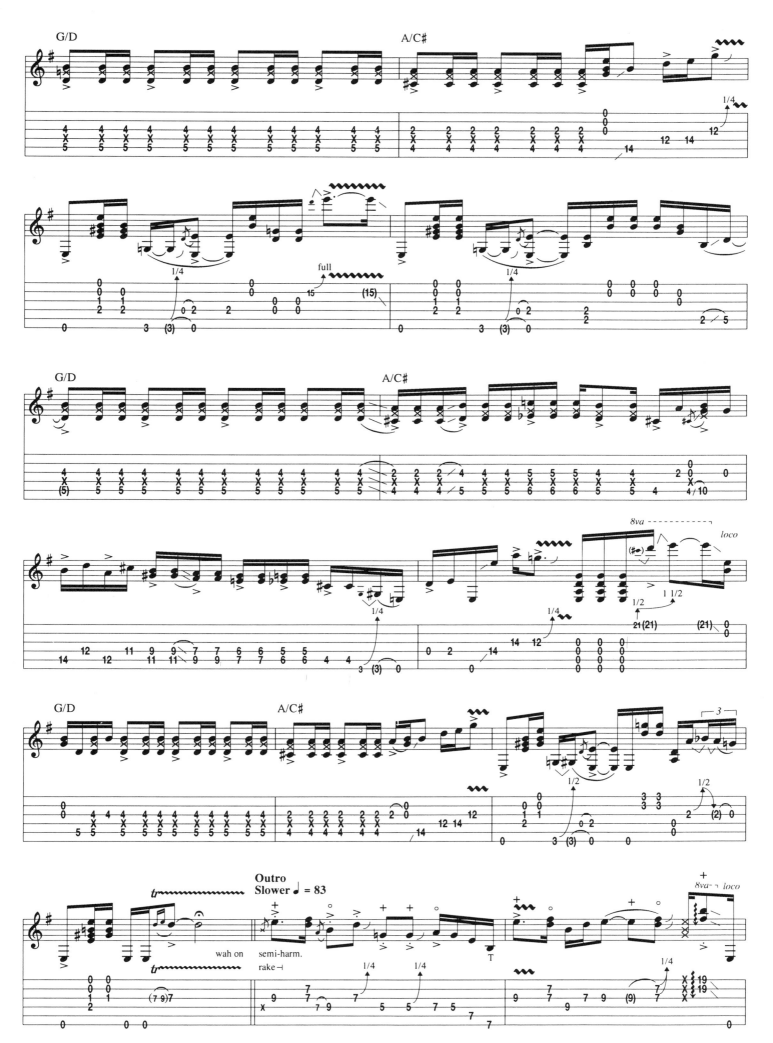

Change It

By Doyle Bramhall

Let's go one more night._____   Get a-way   from the blind_

__ side of life. _   Hon-ey, I want you to   be __   by   my side.   Me 'n' my back

Gtr. 2: w/ Rhy. Fill 1, 2nd time

door_ moves_ ain't _ no _ more,_____   nnn, no   more.   nnn, no   more. _

Guitar Solo

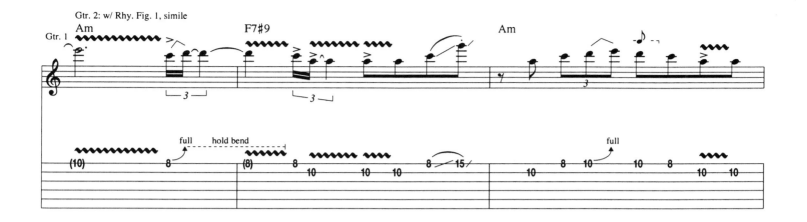

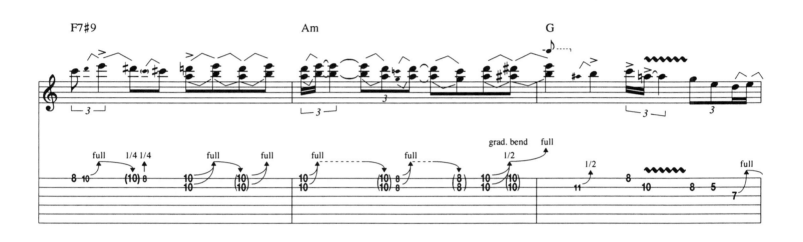

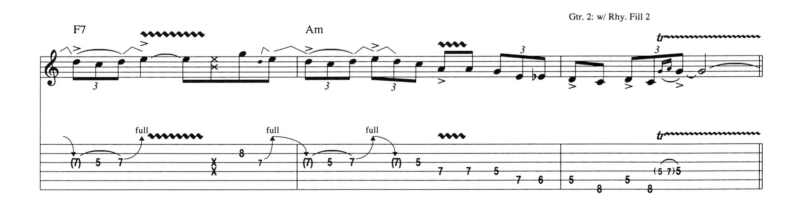

Bridge

Get a - way from the blind - side of life, _ hon - ey, I want ya ta be ___ by my side.

D.S. al Coda

Me 'n' my back door _ moves _ ain't _ no _ more, _____ nnn, no more. _

Coda

Come to me,

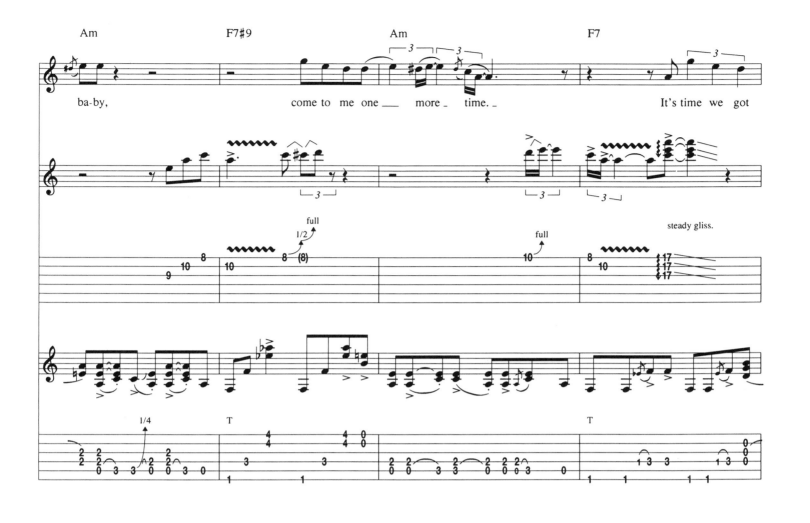

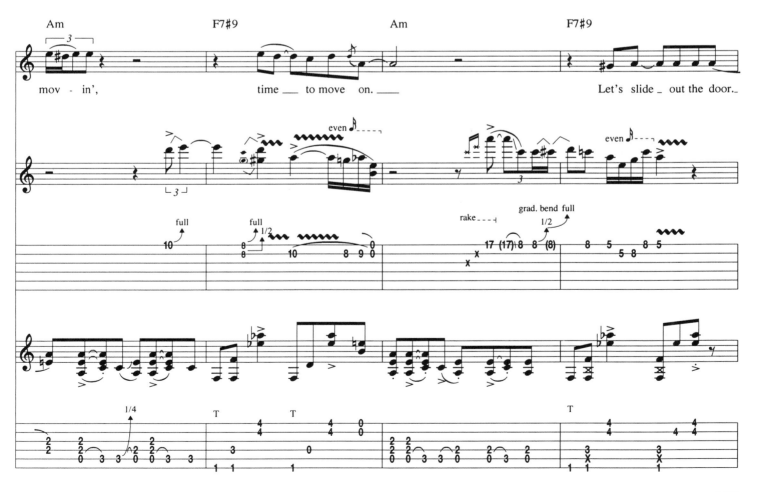

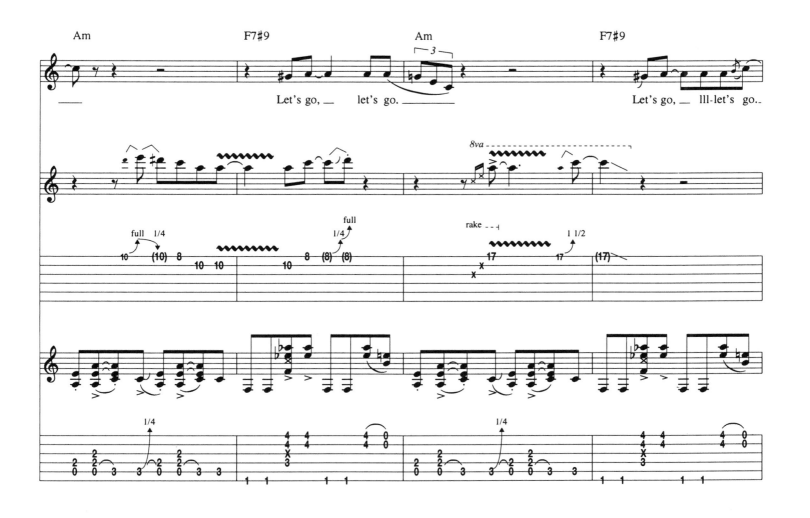

Let's go, — let's go. _____   Let's go, — Ill-let's go...

I've come back for mo'.

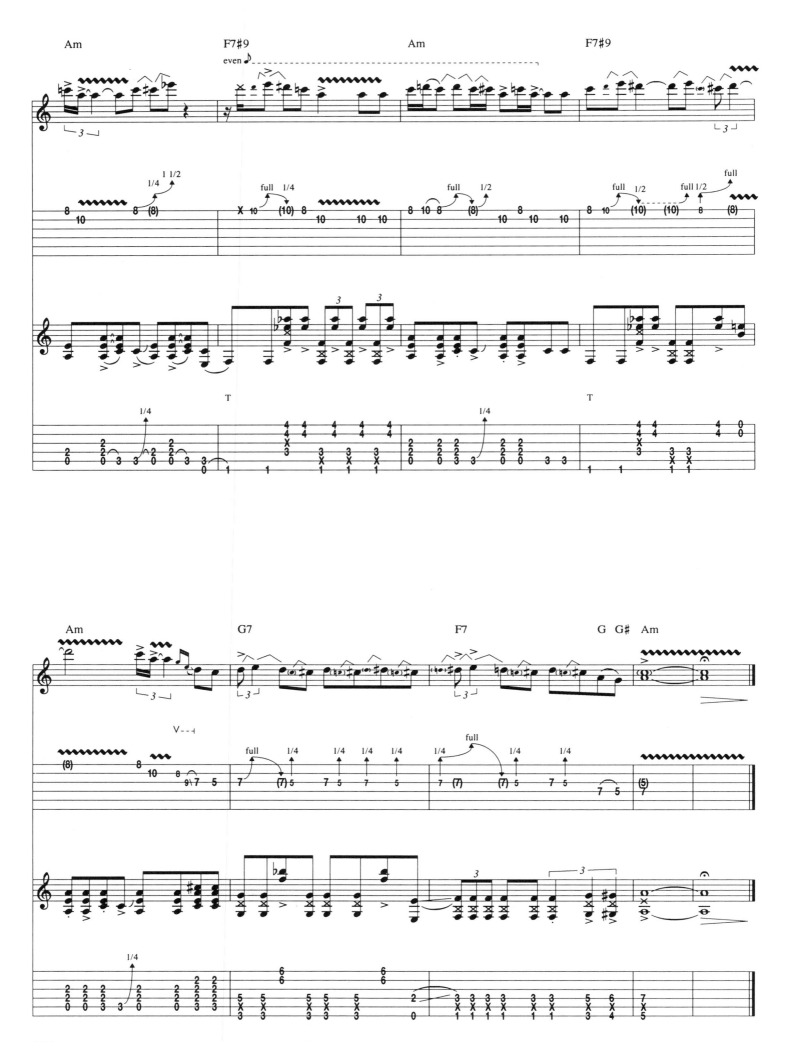

Come On (Part III)

Words and Music by Earl King

Tune Down 1/2 Step:

① = Eb   ④ = Db

② = Bb   ⑤ = Ab

③ = Gb   ⑥ = Eb

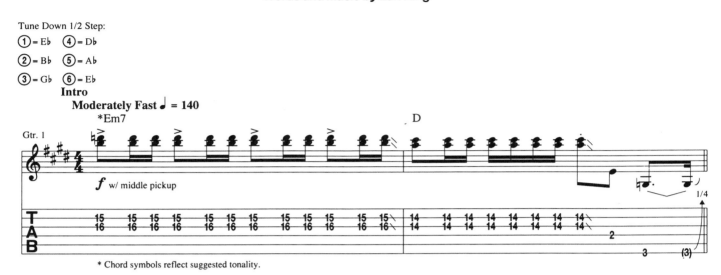

* Chord symbols reflect suggested tonality.

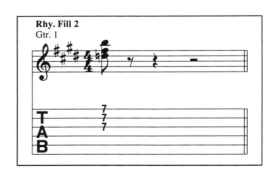

love you so. _____ I love you ba - by, like a   min - er loves gold. ____
up their sleeve. ____   My lov - in' ba - by, ain't the   kind that folds. ____
feel __ so good. ____   You got me flip - pin' like a   flag on a pole. ____

To Coda ⊕

Come on _____ ba - by, let the   good times ah roll.
Come on _____ ba - by, let the   good times ah roll.
Come on _____ sug - ar, let the   good times ah roll. ____

Chorus

Ah, let the   good times   roll. _____
Ah, let the   good times   roll. _____

* Thumb on ⑥

Rhy. Fill 1
Gtr. 1

112

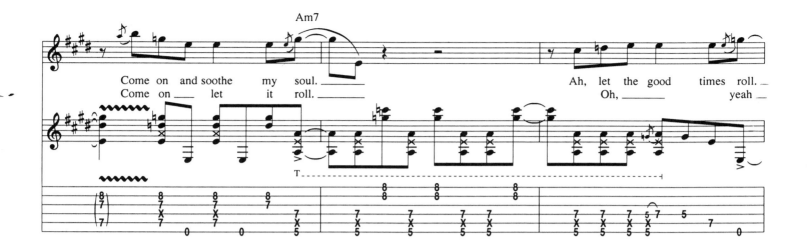

Come on and soothe my soul.
Come on ___ let it roll. ___

Ah, let the good times roll. ___
Oh, ___ yeah ___

Gtr. 1: w/ Riff A, 2nd time

Em7   Bm7

Come on, ___   come on, ___
Let it roll. ___   Come on, ___

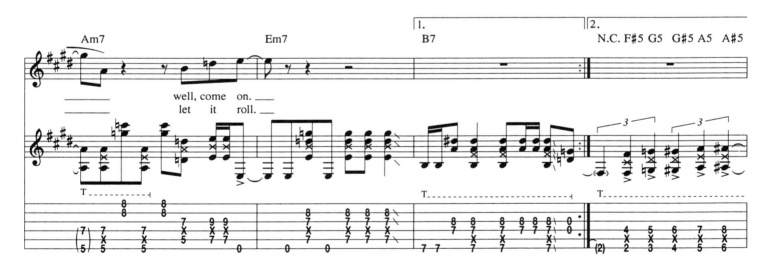

Am7   Em7   B7   N.C. F#5 G5 G#5 A5 A#5

well, come on. ___
let it roll. ___

Riff A
Gtr. 1

Come on, _____ come on, _____

Come on an' let it roll. _____

Outro Solo

switch to
bridge pickup

Gone Home

by Eddie Harris

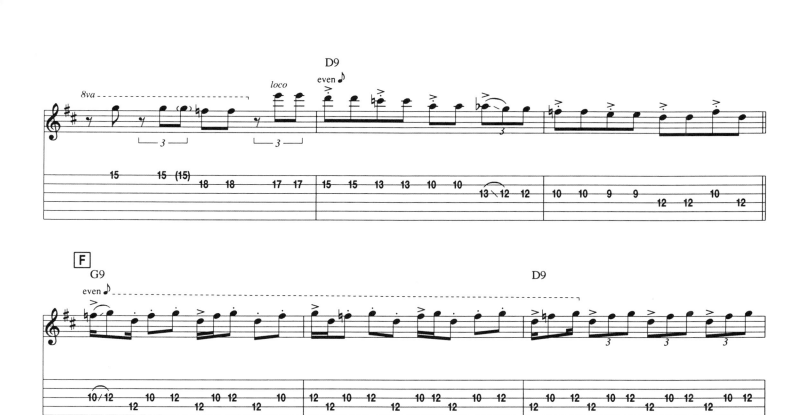

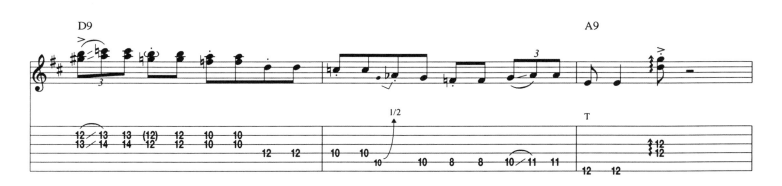

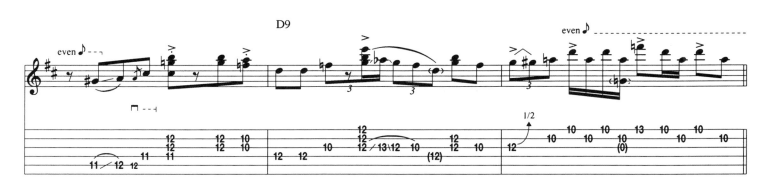

Life Without You

By Stevie Ray Vaughan

you   and the   way

you grin.   The day is nec-es-sar — y

ev-'ry now _ and then, _   for souls to move _ on, _

giv in'-life back a - gain. _   Ah, ___

Fly on, fly on, ___   fly on my friend. _   Go ___ on, ___

live ___ a - gain, _   love a - gain. _   2. Day af - ter day, _

love   you passed __ our   way. __

The an - gels have wait - ed _____   for so long. __

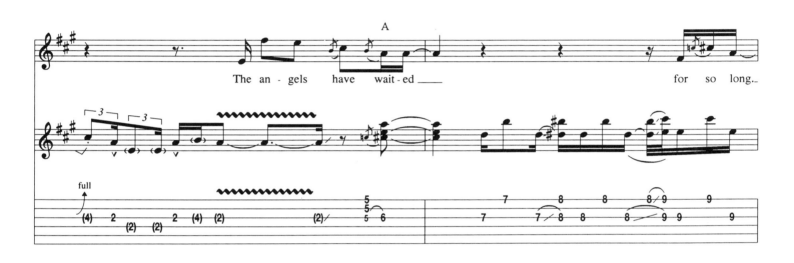

___   Now they   have __ their way. __   Take your place.

Gtr. 2

Gtr. 1

Look At Little Sister

By Hank Ballard

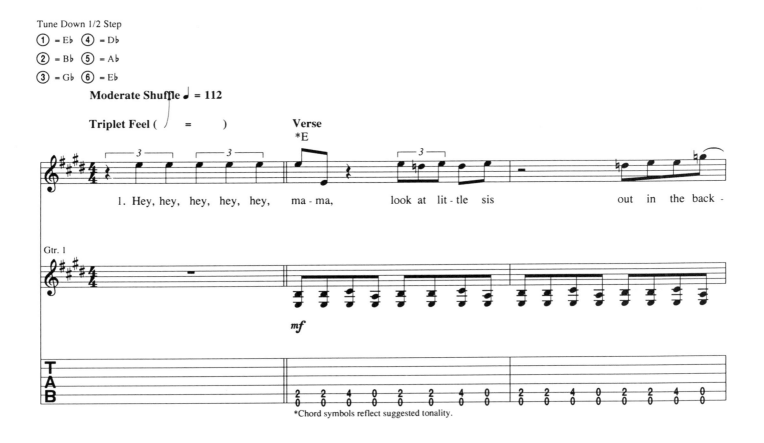

*Chord symbols reflect suggested tonality.

look at lit-tle sis - ter, hey. _____ Hey, hey,

hey, hey, _ look at lit-tle sis - ter.

*Bass plays B on this & all subsequent B7 chords.

Verse

2. What a-bout the neigh - bors, what they gon-na say? _

Stop lit-tle sis - ter get-ting car - ried a - way. Hey, hey, hey,

look at lit-tle sis - ter, hey. _____ Hey, hey,

hey, hey. _ Look at lit-tle sis - ter.

Sax Solo

138

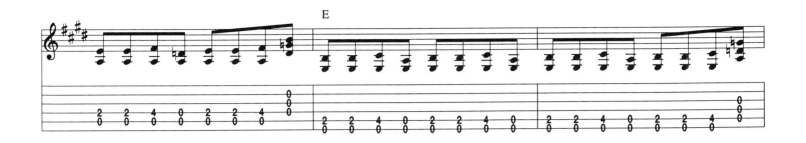

Verse

Lookin' Out The Window

By Doyle Bramhall

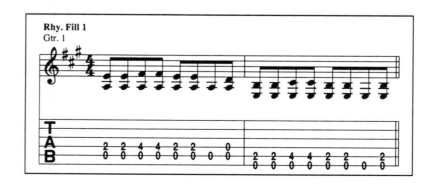

dream - in' all the sweet dreams_ and the mem - 'ries _ of the past.
pick - in' up the piec - es off the shelf. _

Feel so fine, hon - ey, that's
Won't take so long ba -by, 'cause they've

why _ our love should last.
hard-ly _ an - y left.

Feel so good, ba - by, 'n' it's all _ be-cause of you.

I got - ta love _ ya,

I need to love _ ya.

I wan - na love ya so nice. _

Rhy. Fill 2
Gtr. 1

You'll Be Mine

By Willie Dixon

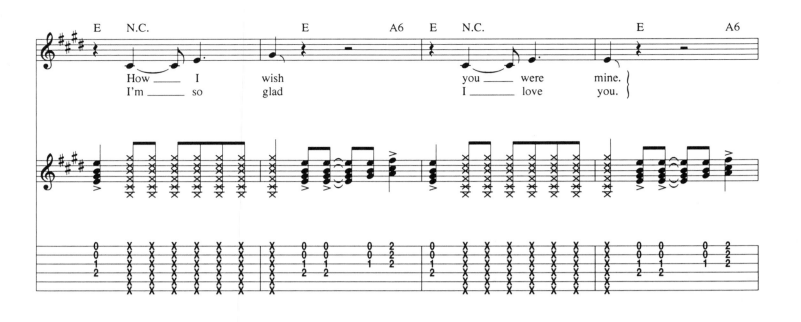

How ___ I   wish   you ___ were   mine.
I'm ___ so   glad   I ___ love   you.

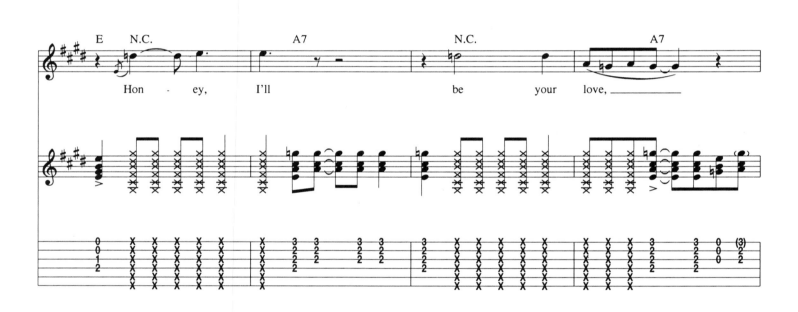

Hon - ey,   I'll   be   your   love, _____

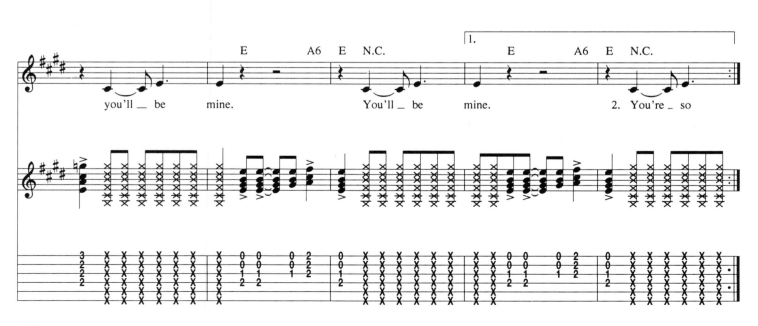

you'll __ be   mine.   You'll __ be   mine.   2. You're _ so

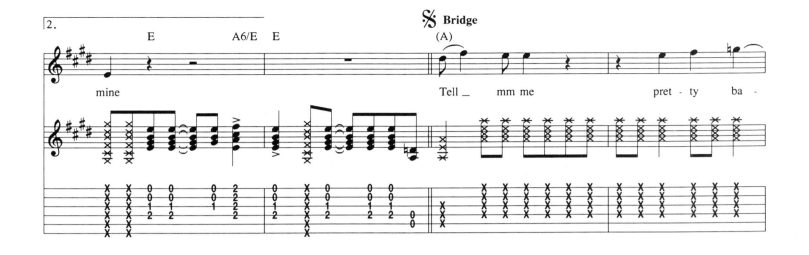

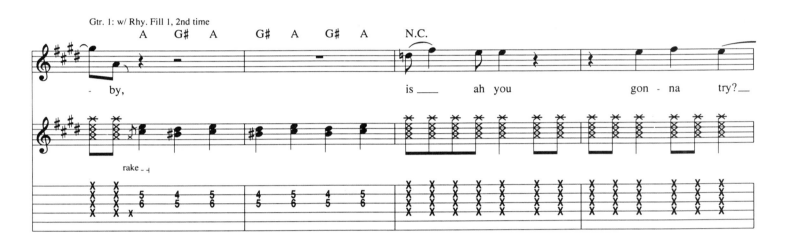

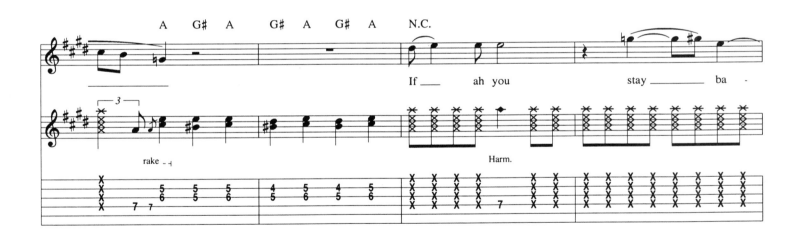

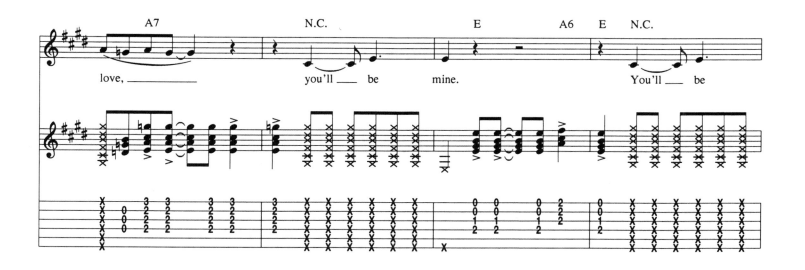

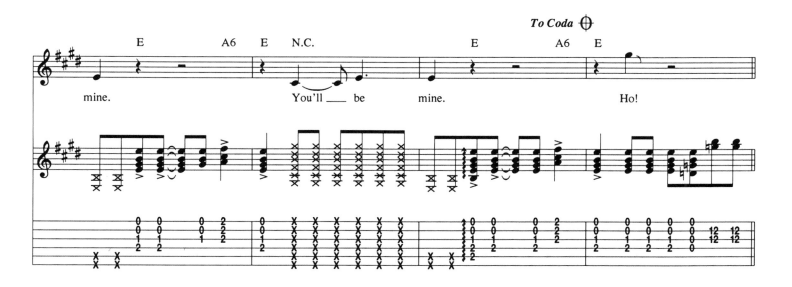

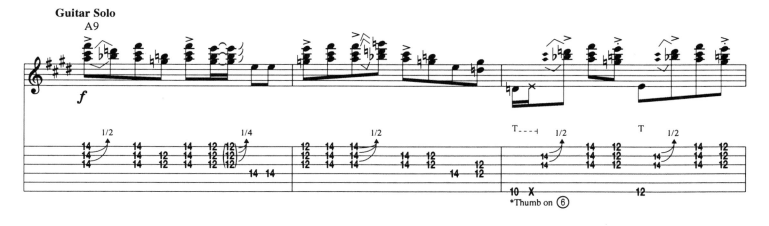

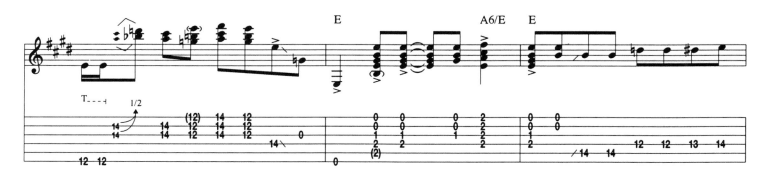

D.S. al Coda

155

Ain't Gone 'N' Give Up On Love

by Stevie Ray Vaughan

Tune Down 1/2 Step:

① =E♭ ④ =D♭
② =B♭ ⑤ =A♭
③ =G♭ ⑥ =E♭

Intro
Slow Blues ♩. = 48

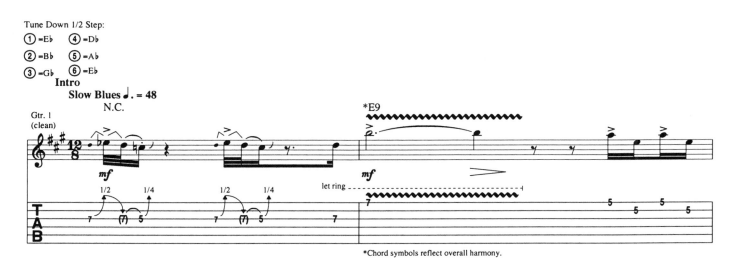

*Chord symbols reflect overall harmony.

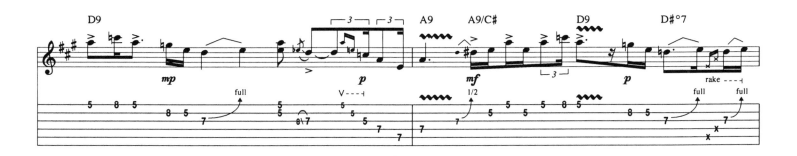

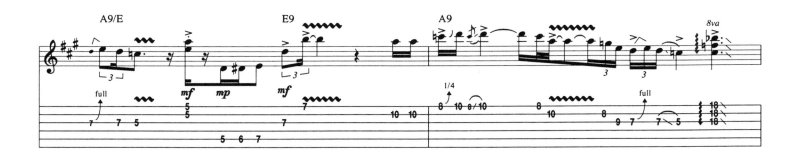

**Note on ① is struck by finger used in previous pull off.

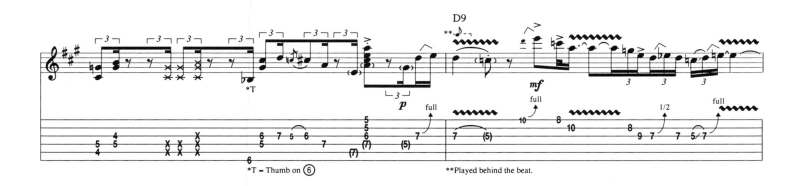

*T = Thumb on ⑥   **Played behind the beat.

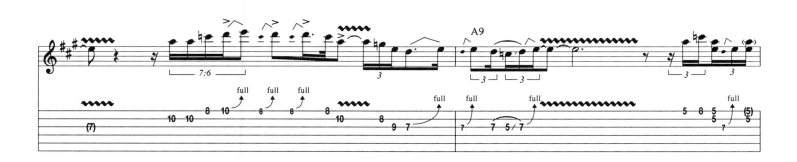

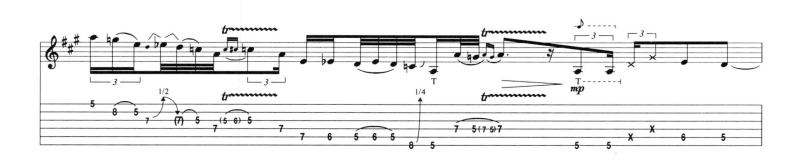

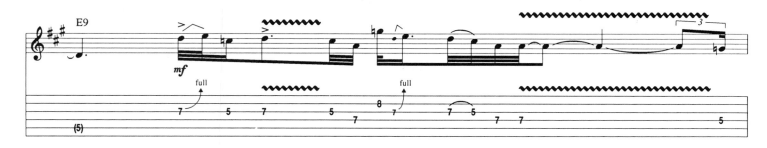

158

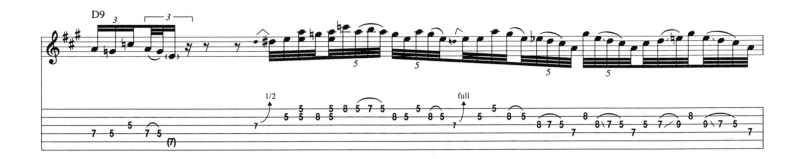

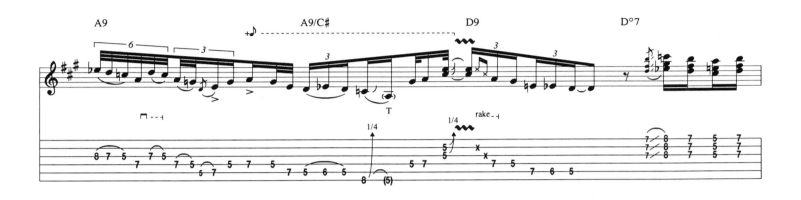

Verse

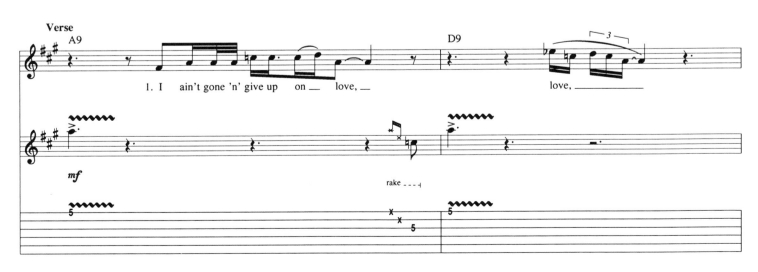

1. I ain't gone 'n' give up on — love, _____ love, _____

ain't gone, ain't gone 'n' give up on

— me.

D9

I ain't gone 'n' give up on _ love, __ love, _____ just ain't gon'

A9

give up on _____ me.

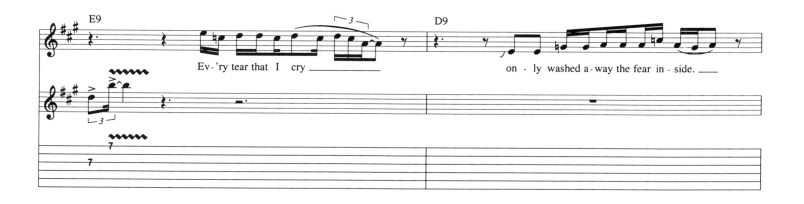

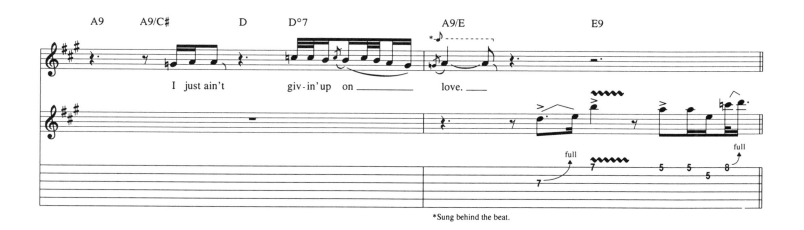

*Sung behind the beat.

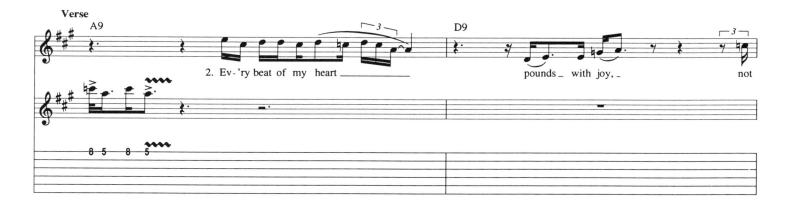

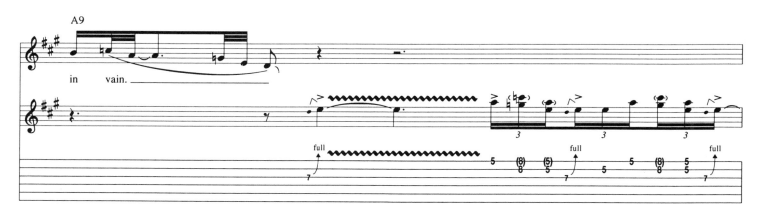

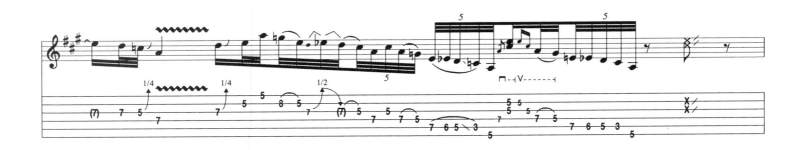

Ev-'ry beat of my heart _____ pounds with joy, _____

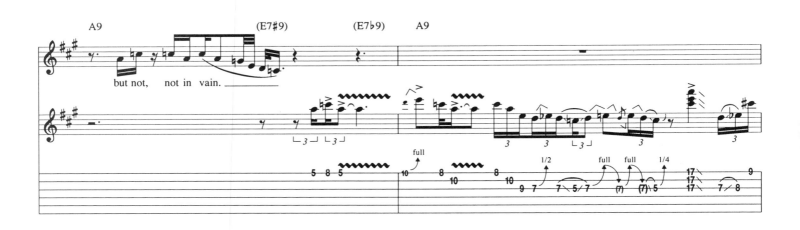

but not, not in vain. _____

And all those ah pain-ful __ mem-o - ries _____ on - ly brought me to my knees. __

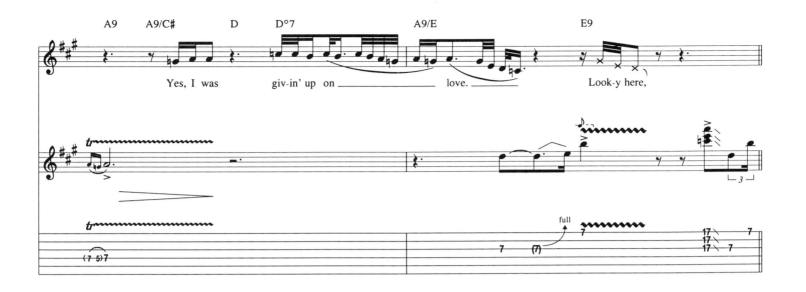

Yes, I was giv-in' up on ___ love. ___ Look-y here,

Bridge

Lit-tle John-ny Tay-lor ___ told me so, aw, ___ so long a-go,

all a-bout_the mid-night cry'n, ___ now, whoa,_ whoa, whoa, _____ all the cheat-in' 'n' lyin'.

Guitar Solo

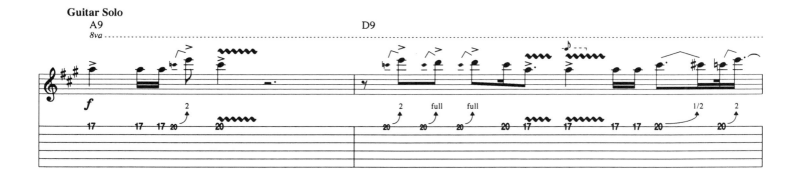

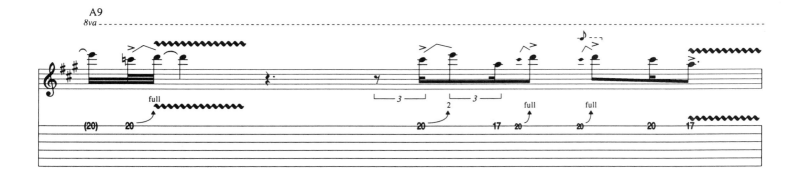

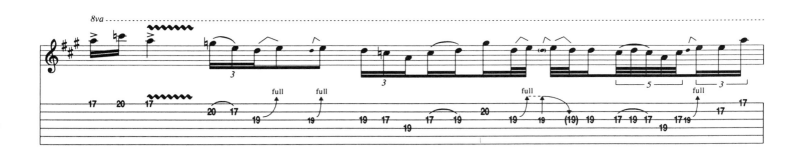

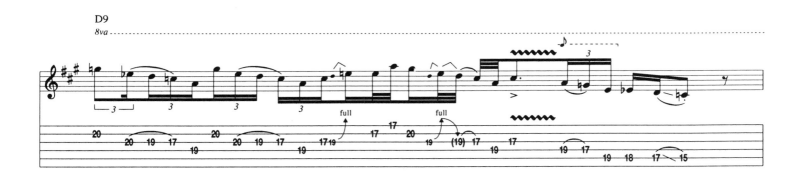

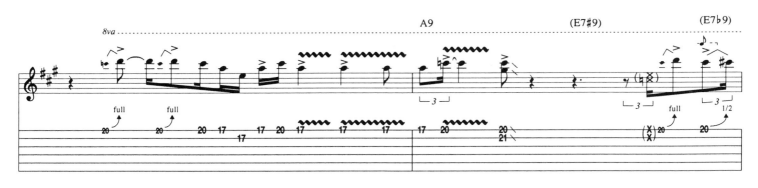

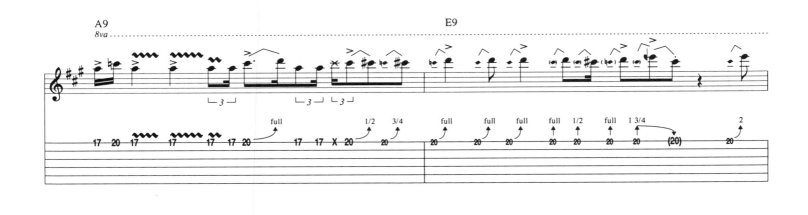

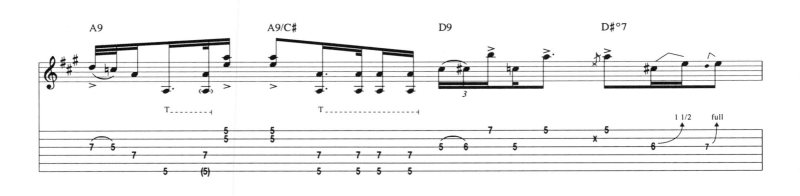

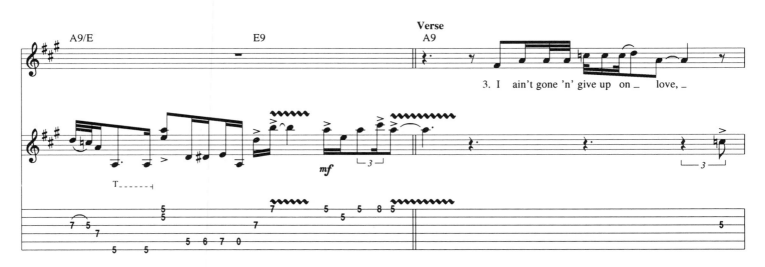

3. I ain't gone 'n' give up on __ love, __

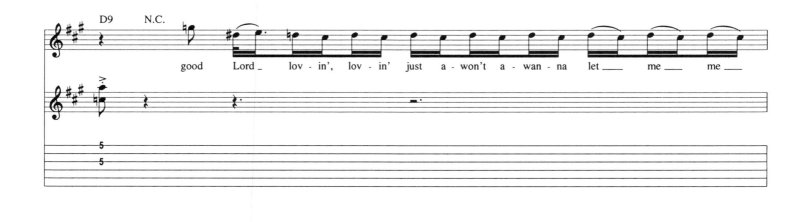

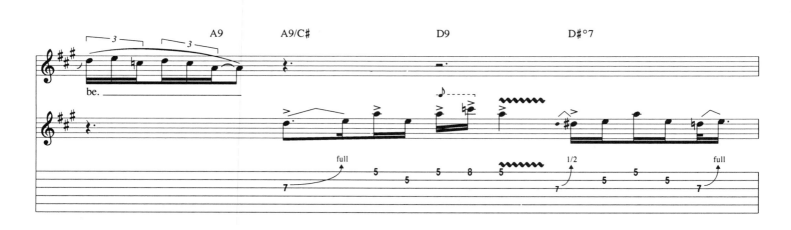

Free Time

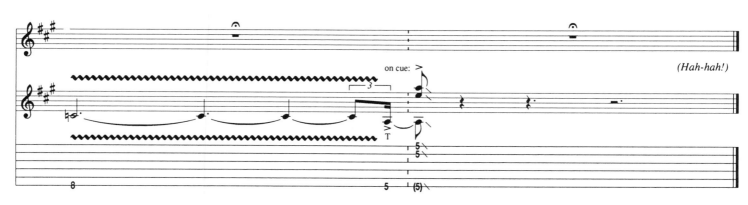

I'm Leaving You (To Commit A Crime)

By Chester Burnett

be - fore I com - mit a crime. ___

You e - vil - est wom - an,

I think e - ver crossed my mind. ___

Verse

2. You put poi - son in my cof - fee,

in - stead of milk or cream. ___

You mixed my drinks

with a can o' red dev-il lye.

Then ya sat right down,

Ba - by, it _____ was not my time.

Guitar Solo
N.C.(Em7)

*Played behind the beat.

*Bend open 5th string behind nut.

Say What

By Stevie Ray Vaughan

* Vibrato bumps ③

Superstition

Words and Music by Stevie Wonder

Tune Down 1/2 Step:

① =Eb ④ =Db
② =Bb ⑤ =Ab
③ =Gb ⑥ =Eb

Intro
Moderately Fast ♩ = 95

1. Ve - ry sup - er - sti -

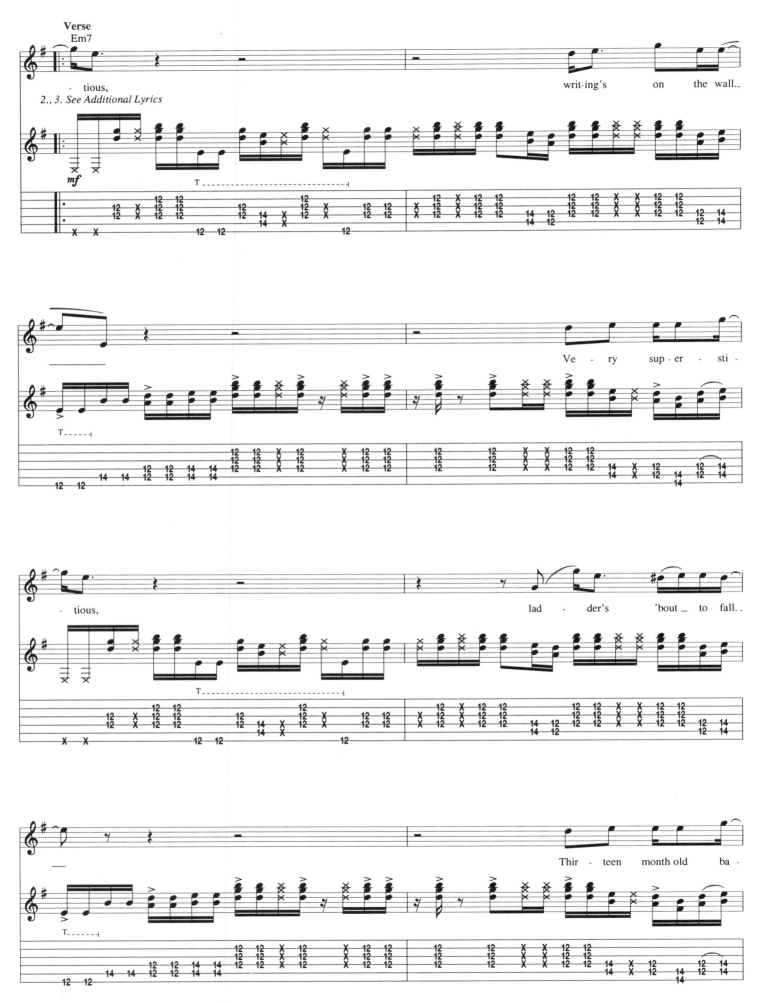

don't un-der-stand, _____ then you suf-fer. _____

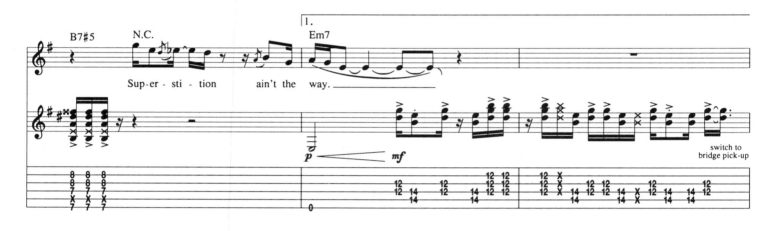

Sup-er-sti-tion ain't the way. _____

switch to
bridge pick-up

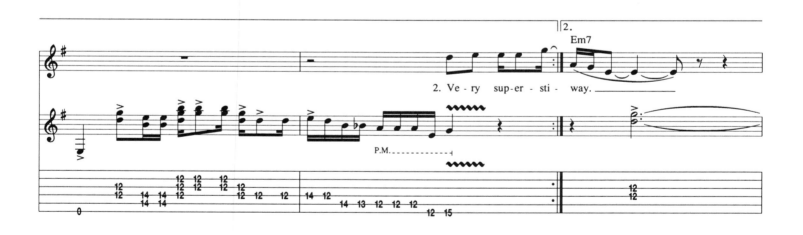

2. Ve-ry sup-er-sti- way. _____

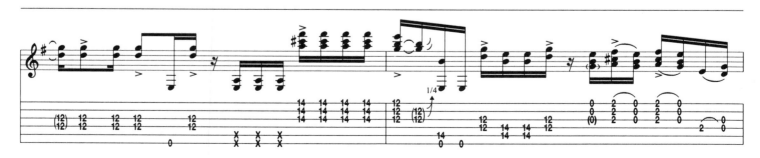

3. Ver - ry sup-er - sti - way. _____

Guitar Solo

194

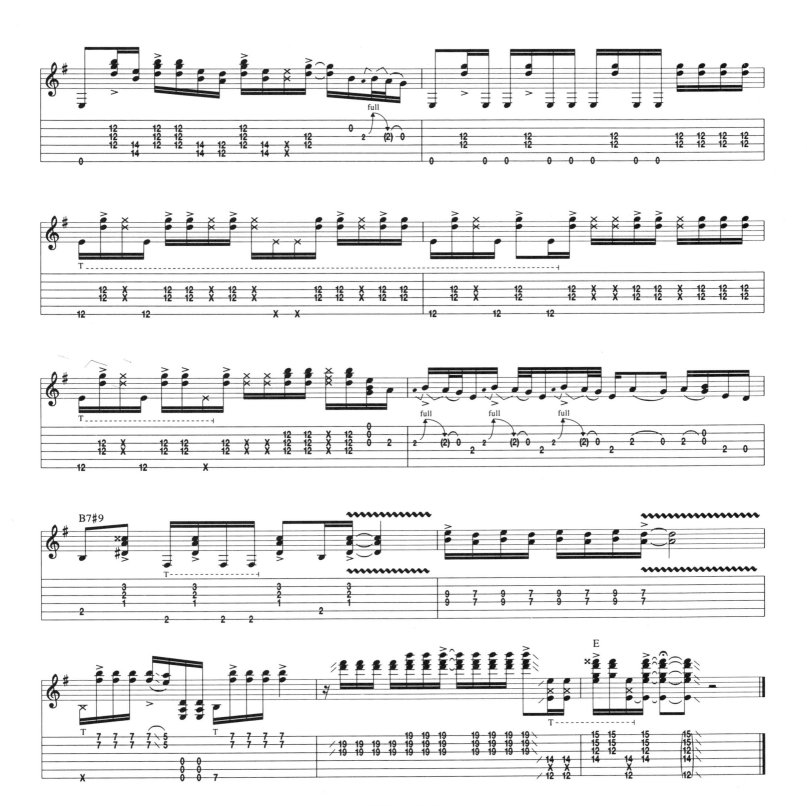

Additional Lyrics

2. Very superstitious, wash your face and hands.
   Rid me of the problem, do all that you can.
   Keep me in a daydream, keep me goin' strong.
   You don't wanna save me, sad is my song.
   When you believe in things that you don't understand, you will suffer.
   Superstition ain't the way.

3. Very superstitious, nothing more to say.
   Very superstitious, devil's on his way.
   Thirteen month old baby, broke the looking glass.
   Seven years of bad luck, good things in the past.
   When you believe in things that you don't understand, you will suffer.
   Superstition ain't the way.

Willy The Wimp

Words and Music by Bill Carter and Ruth Ellen Ellsworth

Tune Down 1/2 Step:

① = Eb ④ = Db

② = Bb ⑤ = Ab

③ = Gb ⑥ = Eb

Intro

Moderately Fast ♩ = 136

* Key signature denotes A Dorian.

* Played ahead of the beat.

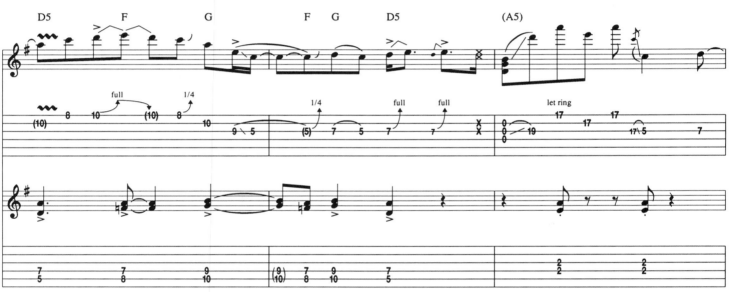

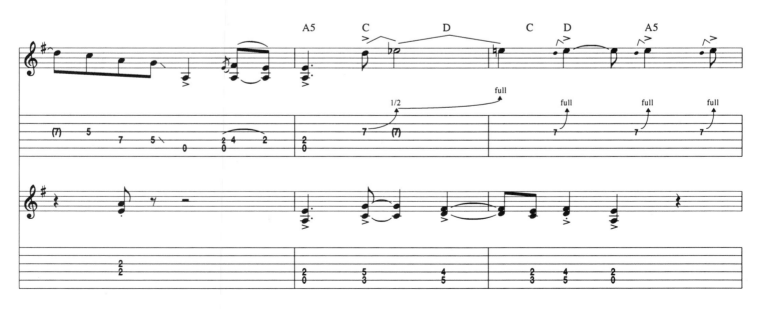

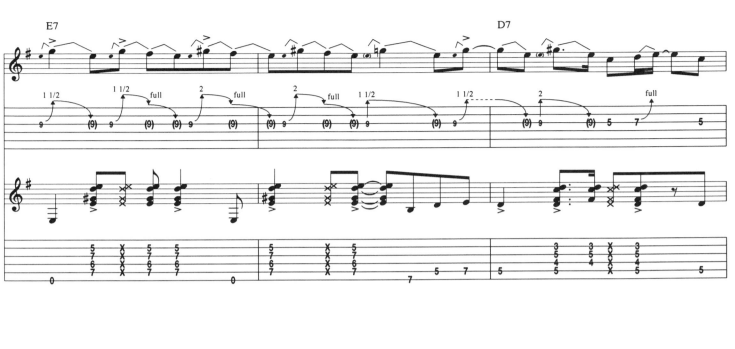

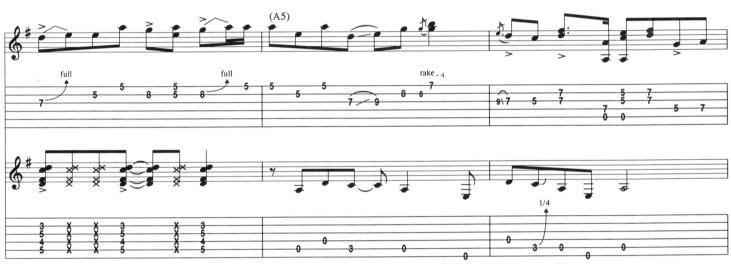

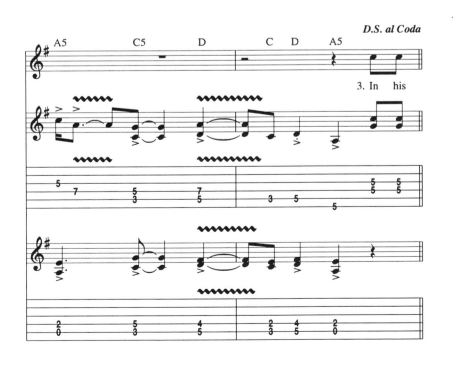

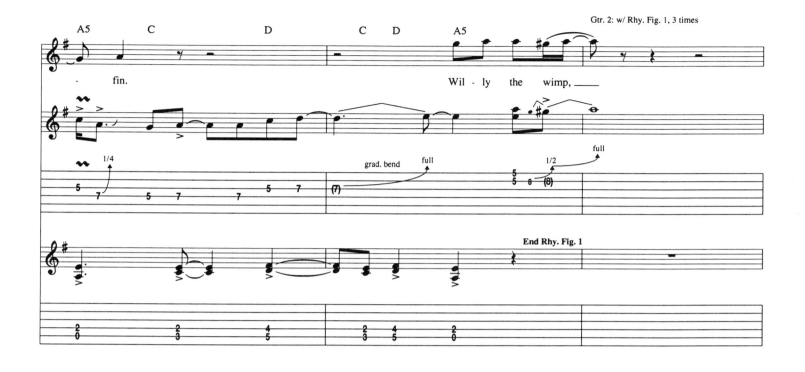

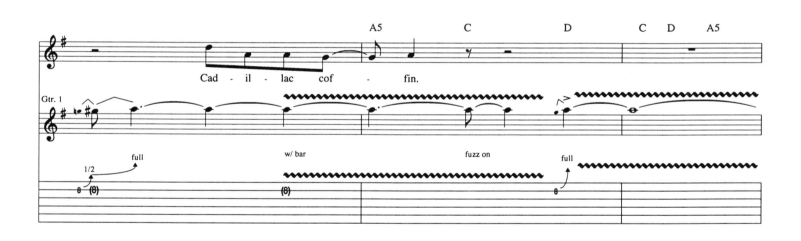

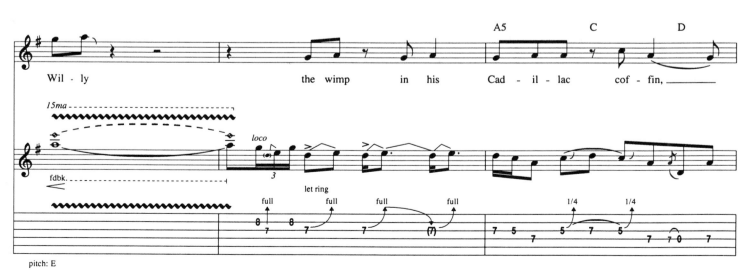

pitch: E

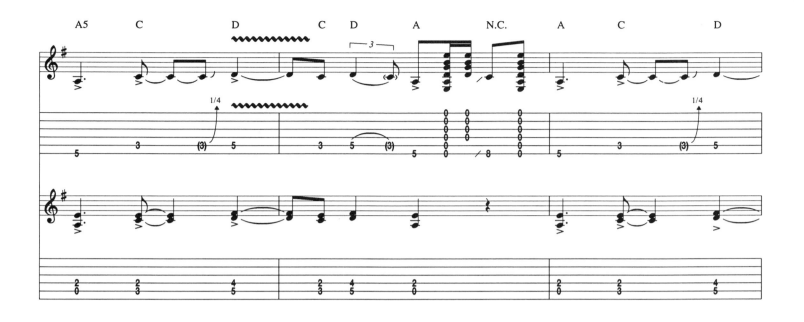

Additional Lyrics

2. That casket, it looked like a fine Seville,
   He had a vanity license and a Cadillac 'ville.
   Willy was propped up in the driver's seat,
   He had diamonds on his fingers and a smile too sweet.
   Fine red suit, had the whole town talkin',
   Willy the wimp in his Cadillac coffin.
   Yeah, Willy the wimp in his Cadillac coffin.

3. In his Cadillac to heaven, he was wavin' the banner.
   He left like he lived; in a lively manner.
   With a hundred dollar bills in his fingers tight.
   He had flowers for wheels and a-flashin' headlights.
   He'd been wishin' for wings; no way he was walkin'.
   Talkin' 'bout a-Willy the wimp in his Cadillac coffin.
   Yeah, Willy the wimp in his Cadillac coffin.

Pipeline

Words and Music by Bob Spickard and Brian Carman

* Chord symbols reflect implied tonality.

* T = Thumb on ⑥

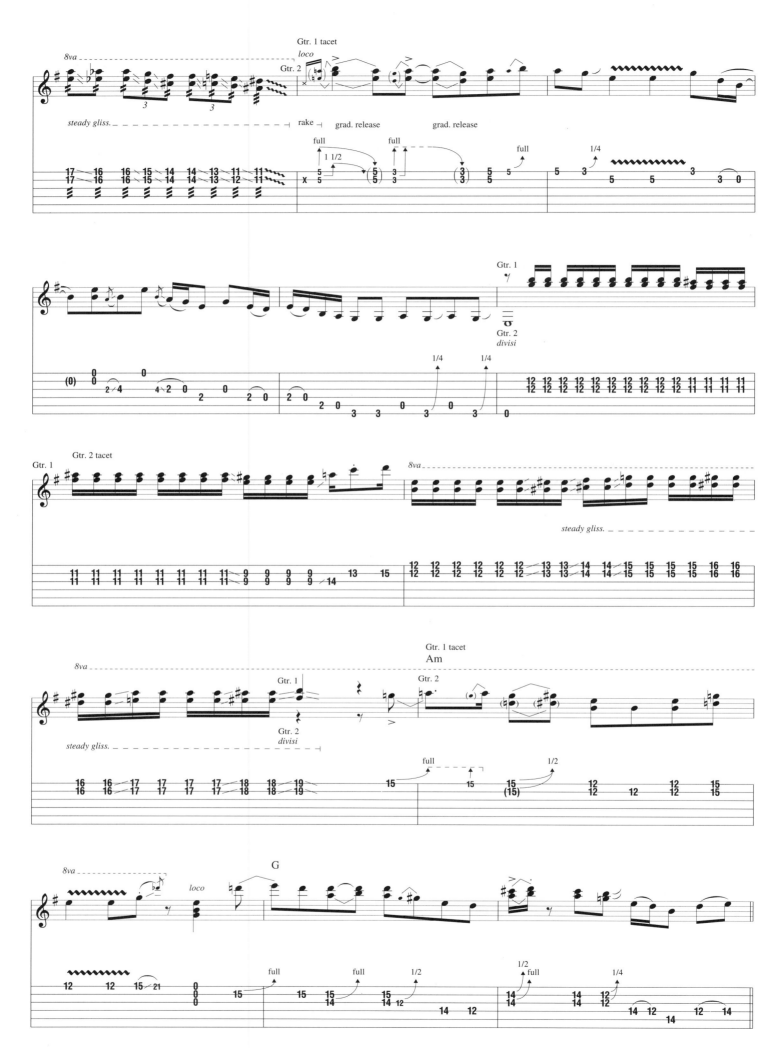

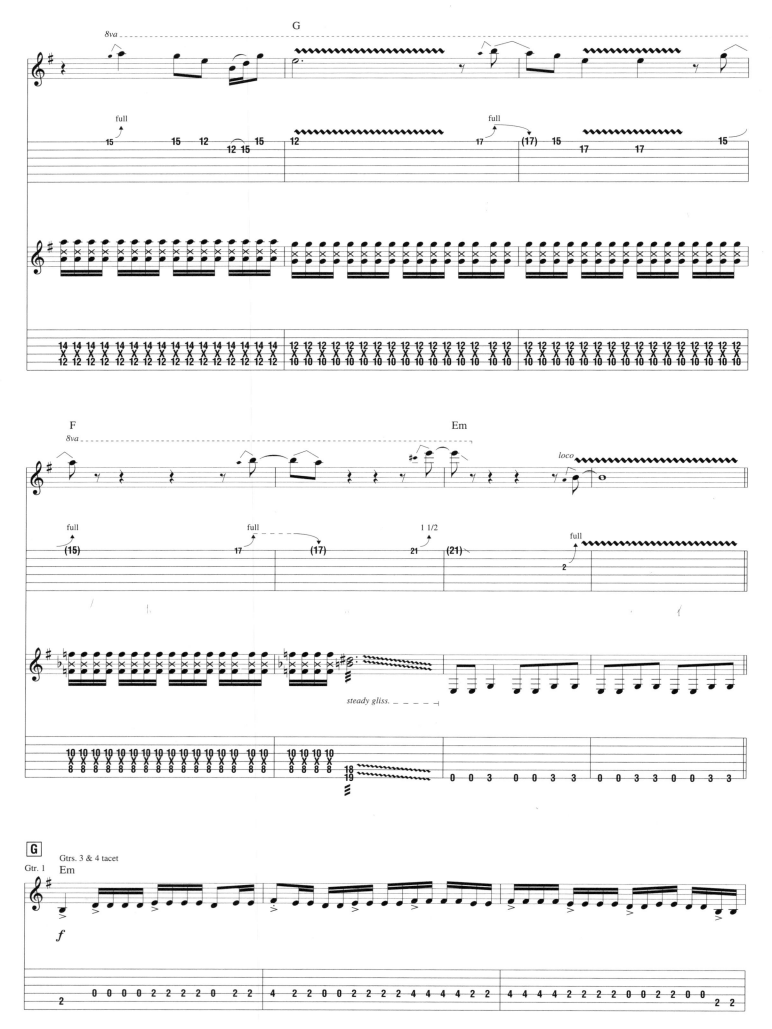

Guitar Notation Legend

Guitar Music can be notated three different ways: on a *musical staff*, in *tablature*, and in *rhythm slashes*.

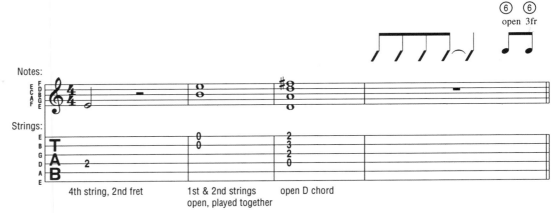

RHYTHM SLASHES are written above the staff. Strum chords in the rhythm indicated. Use the chord diagrams found at the top of the first page of the transcription for the appropriate chord voicings. Round noteheads indicate single notes.

THE MUSICAL STAFF shows pitches and rhythms and is divided by bar lines into measures. Pitches are named after the first seven letters of the alphabet.

TABLATURE graphically represents the guitar fingerboard. Each horizontal line represents a a string, and each number represents a fret.

4th string, 2nd fret

1st & 2nd strings open, played together

open D chord

Definitions for Special Guitar Notation

HALF-STEP BEND: Strike the note and bend up 1/2 step.

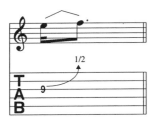

WHOLE-STEP BEND: Strike the note and bend up one step.

GRACE NOTE BEND: Strike the note and bend up as indicated. The first note does not take up any time.

SLIGHT (MICROTONE) BEND: Strike the note and bend up 1/4 step.

BEND AND RELEASE: Strike the note and bend up as indicated, then release back to the original note. Only the first note is struck.

PRE-BEND: Bend the note as indicated, then strike it.

PRE-BEND AND RELEASE: Bend the note as indicated. Strike it and release the bend back to the original note.

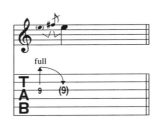

UNISON BEND: Strike the two notes simultaneously and bend the lower note up to the pitch of the higher.

VIBRATO: The string is vibrated by rapidly bending and releasing the note with the fretting hand.

WIDE VIBRATO: The pitch is varied to a greater degree by vibrating with the fretting hand.

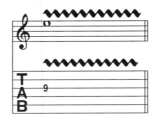

HAMMER-ON: Strike the first (lower) note with one finger, then sound the higher note (on the same string) with another finger by fretting it without picking.

PULL-OFF: Place both fingers on the notes to be sounded. Strike the first note and without picking, pull the finger off to sound the second (lower) note.

LEGATO SLIDE: Strike the first note and then slide the same fret-hand finger up or down to the second note. The second note is not struck.

SHIFT SLIDE: Same as legato slide, except the second note is struck.

TRILL: Very rapidly alternate between the notes indicated by continuously hammering on and pulling off.

TAPPING: Hammer ("tap") the fret indicated with the pick-hand index or middle finger and pull off to the note fretted by the fret hand.

NATURAL HARMONIC: Strike the note while the fret-hand lightly touches the string directly over the fret indicated.

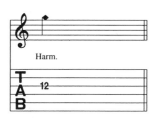

PINCH HARMONIC: The note is fretted normally and a harmonic is produced by adding the edge of the thumb or the tip of the index finger of the pick hand to the normal pick attack.

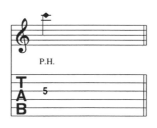

HARP HARMONIC: The note is fretted normally and a harmonic is produced by gently resting the pick hand's index finger directly above the indicated fret (in parentheses) while the pick hand's thumb or pick assists by plucking the appropriate string.

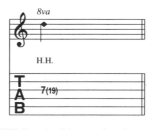

PICK SCRAPE: The edge of the pick is rubbed down (or up) the string, producing a scratchy sound.

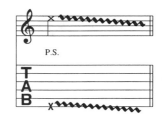

MUFFLED STRINGS: A percussive sound is produced by laying the fret hand across the string(s) without depressing, and striking them with the pick hand.

PALM MUTING: The note is partially muted by the pick hand lightly touching the string(s) just before the bridge.

RAKE: Drag the pick across the strings indicated with a single motion.

TREMOLO PICKING: The note is picked as rapidly and continuously as possible.

ARPEGGIATE: Play the notes of the chord indicated by quickly rolling them from bottom to top.

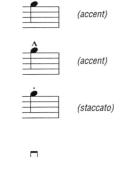

VIBRATO BAR DIVE AND RETURN: The pitch of the note or chord is dropped a specified number of steps (in rhythm) then returned to the original pitch.

VIBRATO BAR SCOOP: Depress the bar just before striking the note, then quickly release the bar.

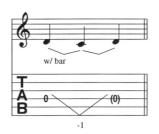

VIBRATO BAR DIP: Strike the note and then immediately drop a specified number of steps, then release back to the original pitch.

Additional Musical Definitions

(accent)	• Accentuate note (play it louder)	
(accent)	• Accentuate note with great intensity	
(staccato)	• Play the note short	
⊓	• Downstroke	
V	• Upstroke	

D.S. al Coda • Go back to the sign (𝄋), then play until the measure marked "**To Coda**," then skip to the section labelled "**Coda**."

D.S. al Fine • Go back to the beginning of the song and play until the measure marked "**Fine**" (end).

Rhy. Fig. • Label used to recall a recurring accompaniment pattern (usually chordal).

Riff • Label used to recall composed, melodic lines (usually single notes) which recur.

Fill • Label used to identify a brief melodic figure which is to be inserted into the arrangement.

Rhy. Fill • A chordal version of a Fill.

tacet • Instrument is silent (drops out).

• Repeat measures between signs.

• When a repeated section has different endings, play the first ending only the first time and the second ending only the second time.

NOTE: Tablature numbers in parentheses mean:
1. The note is being sustained over a system (note in standard notation is tied), or
2. The note is sustained, but a new articulation (such as a hammer-on, pull-off, slide or vibrato begins, or
3. The note is a barely audible "ghost" note (note in standard notation is also in parentheses).

RECORDED VERSIONS
The Best Note-For-Note Transcriptions Available

RECORDED VERSIONS GUITAR

ALL BOOKS INCLUDE TABLATURE

00690016 Will Ackerman Collection	$19.95
00690146 Aerosmith – Toys in the Attic	$19.95
00694865 Alice In Chains – Dirt	$19.95
00694932 Allman Brothers Band – Volume 1	$24.95
00694933 Allman Brothers Band – Volume 2	$24.95
00694934 Allman Brothers Band – Volume 3	$24.95
00694877 Chet Atkins – Guitars For All Seasons	$19.95
00690418 Best of Audio Adrenaline	$17.95
00694918 Randy Bachman Collection	$22.95
00690366 Bad Company Original Anthology - Bk 1	$19.95
00690367 Bad Company Original Anthology - Bk 2	$19.95
00694880 Beatles – Abbey Road	$19.95
00694863 Beatles – Sgt. Pepper's Lonely Hearts Club Band	$19.95
00690383 Beatles – Yellow Submarine	$19.95
00690174 Beck – Mellow Gold	$17.95
00690346 Beck – Mutations	$19.95
00690175 Beck – Odelay	$17.95
00694884 The Best of George Benson	$19.95
00692385 Chuck Berry	$19.95
00692200 Black Sabbath – We Sold Our Soul For Rock 'N' Roll	$19.95
00690115 Blind Melon – Soup	$19.95
00690305 Blink 182 – Dude Ranch	$19.95
00690028 Blue Oyster Cult – Cult Classics	$19.95
00690219 Blur	$19.95
00690168 Roy Buchanon Collection	$19.95
00690364 Cake – Songbook	$19.95
00690337 Jerry Cantrell – Boggy Depot	$19.95
00690293 Best of Steven Curtis Chapman	$19.95
00690043 Cheap Trick – Best Of	$19.95
00690171 Chicago – Definitive Guitar Collection	$22.95
00690415 Clapton Chronicles – Best of Eric Clapton	$17.95
00690393 Eric Clapton – Selections from Blues	$19.95
00660139 Eric Clapton – Journeyman	$19.95
00694869 Eric Clapton – Live Acoustic	$19.95
00694896 John Mayall/Eric Clapton – Bluesbreakers	$19.95
00690162 Best of the Clash	$19.95
00690166 Albert Collins – The Alligator Years	$16.95
00694940 Counting Crows – August & Everything After	$19.95
00690197 Counting Crows – Recovering the Satellites	$19.95
00694840 Cream – Disraeli Gears	$19.95
00690401 Creed – Human Clay	$19.95
00690352 Creed – My Own Prison	$19.95
00690184 dc Talk – Jesus Freak	$19.95
00690333 dc Talk – Supernatural	$19.95
00660186 Alex De Grassi Guitar Collection	$19.95
00690289 Best of Deep Purple	$17.95
00694831 Derek And The Dominos – Layla & Other Assorted Love Songs	$19.95
00690322 Ani Di Franco – Little Plastic Castle	$19.95
00690187 Dire Straits – Brothers In Arms	$19.95
00690191 Dire Straits – Money For Nothing	$24.95
00695382 The Very Best of Dire Straits – Sultans of Swing	$19.95
00660178 Willie Dixon – Master Blues Composer	$24.95
00690250 Best of Duane Eddy	$16.95
00690349 Eve 6	$19.95
00313164 Eve 6 – Horrorscope	$19.95
00690323 Fastball – All the Pain Money Can Buy	$19.95
00690089 Foo Fighters	$19.95
00690235 Foo Fighters – The Colour and the Shape	$19.95
00690394 Foo Fighters – There Is Nothing Left to Lose	$19.95
00690222 G3 Live – Satriani, Vai, Johnson	$22.95
00694807 Danny Gatton – 88 Elmira St	$19.95
00690438 Genesis Guitar Anthology	$19.95

00690127 Goo Goo Dolls – A Boy Named Goo	$19.95
00690338 Goo Goo Dolls – Dizzy Up the Girl	$19.95
00690117 John Gorka Collection	$19.95
00690114 Buddy Guy Collection Vol. A-J	$22.95
00690193 Buddy Guy Collection Vol. L-Y	$22.95
00694798 George Harrison Anthology	$19.95
00690068 Return Of The Hellecasters	$19.95
00692930 Jimi Hendrix – Are You Experienced?	$24.95
00692931 Jimi Hendrix – Axis: Bold As Love	$22.95
00692932 Jimi Hendrix – Electric Ladyland	$24.95
00690218 Jimi Hendrix – First Rays of the New Rising Sun	$27.95
00690038 Gary Hoey – Best Of	$19.95
00660029 Buddy Holly	$19.95
00660169 John Lee Hooker – A Blues Legend	$19.95
00690054 Hootie & The Blowfish – Cracked Rear View	$19.95
00694905 Howlin' Wolf	$19.95
00690136 Indigo Girls – 1200 Curfews	$22.95
00694938 Elmore James – Master Electric Slide Guitar	$19.95
00690167 Skip James Blues Guitar Collection	$16.95
00694833 Billy Joel For Guitar	$19.95
00694912 Eric Johnson – Ah Via Musicom	$19.95
00690169 Eric Johnson – Venus Isle	$22.95
00694799 Robert Johnson – At The Crossroads	$19.95
00693185 Judas Priest – Vintage Hits	$19.95
00690277 Best of Kansas	$19.95
00690073 B. B. King – 1950-1957	$24.95
00690098 B. B. King – 1958-1967	$24.95
00690444 B.B. King and Eric Clapton – Riding with the King	$19.95
00690134 Freddie King Collection	$17.95
00690157 Kiss – Alive	$19.95
00690163 Mark Knopfler/Chet Atkins – Neck and Neck	$19.95
00690296 Patty Larkin Songbook	$17.95
00690018 Living Colour – Best Of	$19.95
00694845 Yngwie Malmsteen – Fire And Ice	$19.95
00694956 Bob Marley – Legend	$19.95
00690283 Best of Sarah McLachlan	$19.95
00690382 Sarah McLachlan – Mirrorball	$19.95
00690354 Sarah McLachlan – Surfacing	$19.95
00690442 Matchbox 20 – Mad Season	$19.95
00690239 Matchbox 20 – Yourself or Someone Like You	$19.95
00690244 Megadeath – Cryptic Writings	$19.95
00690236 Mighty Mighty Bosstones – Let's Face It	$19.95
00690040 Steve Miller Band Greatest Hits	$19.95
00694802 Gary Moore – Still Got The Blues	$19.95
00694958 Mountain, Best Of	$19.95
00690448 MxPx – The Ever Passing Moment	$19.95
00694913 Nirvana – In Utero	$19.95
00694883 Nirvana – Nevermind	$19.95
00690026 Nirvana – Acoustic In New York	$19.95
00690121 Oasis – (What's The Story) Morning Glory	$19.95
00690204 Offspring, The – Ixnay on the Hombre	$17.95
00690203 Offspring, The – Smash	$17.95
00694830 Ozzy Osbourne – No More Tears	$19.95
00694855 Pearl Jam – Ten	$19.95
00690053 Liz Phair – Whip Smart	$19.95
00690176 Phish – Billy Breathes	$22.95
00690424 Phish – Farmhouse	$19.95
00690331 Phish – The Story of Ghost	$19.95
00690428 Pink Floyd – Dark Side of the Moon	$19.95
00693800 Pink Floyd – Early Classics	$19.95
00690456 P.O.D. – The Fundamental Elements of Southtown	$19.95
00694967 Police – Message In A Box Boxed Set	$70.00
00694974 Queen – A Night At The Opera	$19.95

00690395 Rage Against The Machine – The Battle of Los Angeles	$19.95
00690145 Rage Against The Machine – Evil Empire	$19.95
00690179 Rancid – And Out Come the Wolves	$22.95
00690055 Red Hot Chili Peppers – Bloodsugarsexmagik	$19.95
00690379 Red Hot Chili Peppers – Californication	$19.95
00690090 Red Hot Chili Peppers – One Hot Minute	$22.95
00694937 Jimmy Reed – Master Bluesman	$19.95
00694899 R.E.M. – Automatic For The People	$19.95
00690260 Jimmie Rodgers Guitar Collection	$19.95
00690014 Rolling Stones – Exile On Main Street	$24.95
00690186 Rolling Stones – Rock & Roll Circus	$19.95
00690135 Otis Rush Collection	$19.95
00690031 Santana's Greatest Hits	$19.95
00690150 Son Seals – Bad Axe Blues	$17.95
00690128 Seven Mary Three – American Standards	$19.95
00120105 Kenny Wayne Shepherd – Ledbetter Heights	$19.95
00120123 Kenny Wayne Shepherd – Trouble Is	$19.95
00690196 Silverchair – Freak Show	$19.95
00690130 Silverchair – Frogstomp	$19.95
00690041 Smithereens – Best Of	$19.95
00690385 Sonicflood	$19.95
00694885 Spin Doctors – Pocket Full Of Kryptonite	$19.95
00694921 Steppenwolf, The Best Of	$22.95
00694957 Rod Stewart – Acoustic Live	$22.95
00690021 Sting – Fields Of Gold	$19.95
00690242 Suede – Coming Up	$19.95
00694824 Best Of James Taylor	$16.95
00690238 Third Eye Blind	$19.95
00690403 Third Eye Blind – Blue	$19.95
00690267 311	$19.95
00690030 Toad The Wet Sprocket	$19.95
00690228 Tonic – Lemon Parade	$19.95
00690295 Tool – Aenima	$19.95
00690039 Steve Vai – Alien Love Secrets	$24.95
00690172 Steve Vai – Fire Garden	$24.95
00690023 Jimmie Vaughan – Strange Pleasures	$19.95
00690370 Stevie Ray Vaughan and Double Trouble – The Real Deal: Greatest Hits Volume 2	$22.95
00690455 Stevie Ray Vaughan – Blues at Sunrise	$19.95
00660136 Stevie Ray Vaughan – In Step	$19.95
00690417 Stevie Ray Vaughan – Live at Carnegie Hall	$19.95
00694835 Stevie Ray Vaughan – The Sky Is Crying	$19.95
00694776 Vaughan Brothers – Family Style	$19.95
00120026 Joe Walsh – Look What I Did...	$24.95
00694789 Muddy Waters – Deep Blues	$24.95
00690071 Weezer	$19.95
00690286 Weezer – Pinkerton	$19.95
00690447 Who, The – Best of	$24.95
00694970 Who, The – Definitive Collection A-E	$24.95
00694971 Who, The – Definitive Collection F-Li	$24.95
00694972 Who, The – Definitive Collection Lo-R	$24.95
00694973 Who, The – Definitive Collection S-Y	$24.95
00690319 Stevie Wonder Hits	$17.95

MASTER THE Blues

The Songs and Licks That Made It Happen
by Fred Sokolow
A complete survey of a musical genre, its pioneers and how it developed, including: Six note-for-note transcriptions of famous tunes pivotal to the genre; extensive instruction in the essential playing styles of the genre, using scales, chords, licks, and musical exercises; the history of the development of each playing style; biographies of the pioneering artists; a recording of the songs, exercises, and licks.

With guitar instruction from Hal Leonard
All books include notes and tab.

Inside the Blues 1942-1982
by Dave Rubin

The definitive blues collection! Over 150 pages spanning 40 years of blues history with techniques of the greatest blues guitarists of all time, including T-Bone Walker, Muddy Waters, Elmore James, B.B. King, Otis Rush, Buddy Guy, Albert King, Jimi Hendrix, Johnny Winter, Stevie Ray Vaughan, and many more. Includes instruction and musical examples – an essential volume for any student of the blues!
00696558 ....$24.95

Art of the Shuffle
by Dave Rubin

This method book explores shuffle, boogie and swing rhythms for guitar. Includes tab and notation, and covers Delta, country, Chicago, Kansas City, Texas, New Orleans, West Coast, and bebop blues. Also includes audio for demonstration of each style and to jam along with.
00695005 Book/CD Pack $19.95

Power Trio Blues
by Dave Rubin

This book/CD pack details how to play electric guitar in a trio with bass and drums. Boogie, shuffle, and slow blues rhythms, licks, double stops, chords, and bass patterns are presented for full and exciting blues. A CD with the music examples performed by a smokin' power trio is included for play-along instruction and jamming.
00695028 Book/CD Pack $19.95

Basic Blues for Guitar

The most thorough blues guitar book yet. Over 35 blues tunes covering electric and rock blues, folk, fingerpicking and bottleneck blues, B.B. King and Chuck Berry styles, jazzy blues and more. Plus positions, scales chords, discographies and an overview of styles from Robert Johnson to George Benson. Written in music tablature with chord grids. All tunes are played on the stereo cassette that comes with the book.
00699002 Bk/Cassette Pack.................$16.95

Lead Blues Licks
by Michael P. Wolfsohn

This book examines blues licks in the styles of such greats as B.B. King, Albert King, Stevie Ray Vaughan, Eric Clapton, Chuck Berry, and more. You'll progress from the standard blues progression and blues scale to the various techniques of bending, fast pull offs and hammer-ons, double stops, and more.
00699325...............................$6.95

Acoustic Country Blues
Delta Blues Before Robert Johnson
Inside the Blues
by Dave Rubin

A valuable collection of 12 classic song transcriptions complete with detailed instruction and photos. The songs include: Cross Road Blues (Crossroads) • I Believe I'll Dust My Broom • I'm Gonna Yola My Blues Away • Lead Pencil Blues • Life Saver Blues • Roll and Tumble Blues • You Gonna Need Somebody When You Die • and more.
00695139 Book/CD Pack $16.95

Birth of the Groove
R&B, Soul and Funk Guitar: 1940-1965
by Dave Rubin

The years 1945-1965 saw a radical and exciting shift in American popular music. Blues and swing jazz helped to produce a new musical form called rhythm and blues, which in turn set in motion the development of soul and funk, not to mention rock 'n' roll. This book/CD pack explores everything from the swinging boogie of Tiny Grimes to the sweaty primal funk of Jimmy Nolen, and everyone in between. The CD includes 45 full-band tracks.
00695036 Book/CD Pack $17.95

Electric Slide Guitar
by David Hamburger

This book/audio method explores the basic fundamentals of slide guitar: from selecting a slide and proper setup of the guitar, to open and standard tuning. Plenty of music examples are presented showing sample licks as well as backup/rhythm slide work. Each section also examines techniques and solos in the style of the best slide guitarists, including Duane Allman, Dave Hole, Ry Cooder, Bonnie Raitt, Muddy Waters, Johnny Winter and Elmore James.
00695022 Book/CD Pack $19.95

101 Must-Know Blues Licks
A Quick, Easy Reference for All Guitarists
by Wolf Marshall

Now you can add authentic blues feel and flavor to your playing! Here are 101 definitive licks – plus a demonstration CD – from every major blues guitar style, neatly organized into easy-to-use categories. They're all here, including Delta blues, jump blues, country blues, Memphis blues, Texas blues, West Coast blues, Chicago blues, and British blues.
00695318 Book/CD Pack $14.95

Fretboard Roadmaps Blues Guitar
for Acoustic and Electric Guitar
by Fred Sokolow

These essential fretboard patterns are roadmaps that all great blues guitarists know and use. This book teaches how to: play lead and rhythm anywhere on the fretboard, in any key; play a variety of lead guitar styles; play chords and progressions anywhere on the fretboard, in any key; expand chord vocabulary; learn to think musicially, the way the pros do.
00695350 Book/CD Pack $12.95

12-Bar Blues
by Dave Rubin

The term "12-bar blues" has become synonymous with blues music and is the basis for an incredible body of jazz, rock 'n' roll, and other forms of popular music. This book/CD pack is solely devoted to providing guitarists with all the technical tools necessary for playing 12-bar blues with authority. The CD includes 24 full-band tracks. Covers: boogie, shuffle, swing, riff, and jazzy blues progressions; Chicago, minor, slow, bebop, and other blues styles; soloing, intros, turnarounds, and more.
00695187 Book/CD Pack $14.95

The Roots of Acoustic Blues

Songs include: Baby, Please Don't Go • Come Back Baby • Diddy Wah Diddy • Hey Hey • I'm So Glad.

00699068 Book/CD Pack $14.95

The Roots of Electric Blues

Songs include: The Things I Used to Do • Hideaway • Killing Floor • Mean Old World • I Can't Quit You Baby • Why I Sing the Blues.

00699067 Book/CD Pack $14.95

The Roots of Slide Guitar

Songs include: Come On in My Kitchen • Motherless Children • Roll and Tumble Blues • You Can't Lose What You Ain't Never Had • You Gotta Move • You Shook Me.

00699083 Book/CD Pack $14.95

Blues You Can Use
by John Ganapes

A comprehensive source for learning blues guitar, designed to develop both your lead and rhythm playing. Covers all styles of blues, including Texas, Delta, R&B, early rock and roll, gospel, blues/rock and more. Includes 21 complete solos; extensive instruction; audio with leads and full band backing; and more!
00695007 Book/CD Pack....................$19.95

Blues You Can Use Book of Guitar Chords
by John Ganapes

A reference guide to blues, R&B, jazz, and rock rhythm guitar, with hundreds of voicings, chord theory construction, chord progressions and exercises and much more. The Blues You Can Use Book Of Guitar Chords is useful for the beginner to advanced player.
00695082................................$14.95

More Blues You Can Use
by John Ganapes

A complete guide to learning blues guitar, covering scales, rhythms, chords, patterns, rakes, techniques, and more. CD includes 13 full-demo solos.
00695165 Book/CD Pack $19.95

Blues Licks You Can Use
by John Ganapes

Contains music and performance notes for 75 hot lead phrases, covering styles including up-tempo and slow blues, jazz-blues, shuffle blues, swing blues and more! CD features full-band examples.
00695386 Book/CD Pack $14.95

FOR MORE INFORMATION, SEE YOUR LOCAL MUSIC DEALER,
OR WRITE TO:

7777 W. BLUEMOUND RD. P.O. BOX 13819 MILWAUKEE, WI 53213

Prices, availability, and contents subject to change without notice. Some products may not be available outside the U.S.A.

1 2 MAR 2020		
1 2 JUL 2022		